SO-AJL-378

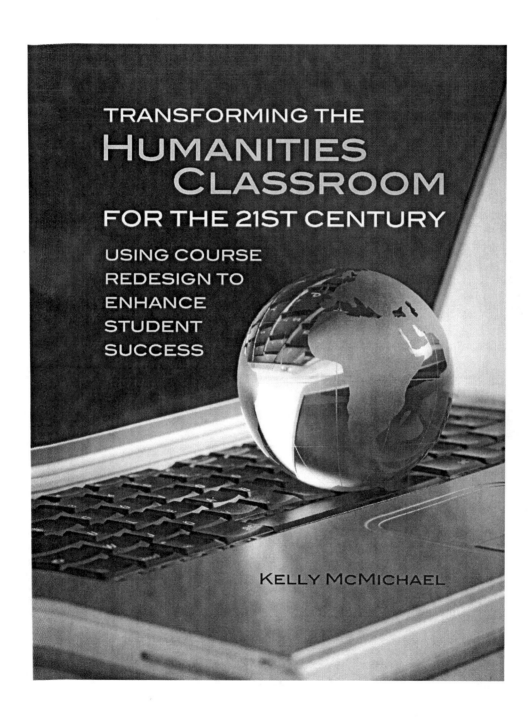

TRANSFORMING THE HUMANITIES CLASSROOM

FOR THE 21ST CENTURY

USING COURSE REDESIGN TO ENHANCE STUDENT SUCCESS

KELLY McMICHAEL

Copyright © 2009 by Bent Tree Press.

All rights reserved. No part of this book may be reproduced in
any form whatsoever, by photograph or xerography or by any
other means, by broadcast or transmission, by translation into
any kind of language, nor by recording electronically or
otherwise, without permission in writing from the publisher,
except by a reviewer, who may quote brief passages in critical
articles and reviews.

Printed in the United States of America.

ISBN: 1-60250-191-2
         978-1-60250-191-1

Bent Tree Press

59 Damonte Ranch Parkway, Suite B284 • Reno, NV 89521 • (800) 970-1883

www.benttreepress.com

Address all correspondence and order information to the above address.

TABLE OF CONENTS

A C K N O W L E D G E M E N T S

Writing a book is always a communal activity and this project has been no different. As mentioned in the text, Cynthia Beard, Denise Baxter, Kelly Donahue-Wallace, and Tracey Gau have generously provided me with reports, documents, and their time, from which to craft summaries of the courses that they have redesigned.

Dr. Philip Turner has been my boss, mentor, and inspiration throughout the N-Gen Course Redesign Project™, and his vision has led our team of staff and faculty to heights not otherwise obtainable. Other staff at CLEAR—Jennifer Phillips, Teresa Cox, Ron Carriveau, and Bill Watson—have patiently knocked on my office door when I was hibernating with this manuscript. For their patience, insight, and constant inspiration, I am truly grateful.

Finally, I would like to thank my children and husband for bearing with me during long evenings spent at the computer instead of in their company. Thank you Jahue, Ryan, and Emma for being so understanding!

INTRODUCTION

The 21st Century Classroom

I shuffled into the ballroom late and scanned the space, looking for an empty seat. I'd never heard of the Croquet Project, Julian Lombardi, or David Reed, but I was intrigued as were, apparently, the hundred or so other folks who had crowded into the hotel's meeting space to hear the plenary session at the 11th annual Sloan-C International Conference on Asynchronous Learning Networks. The chatter ceased as the room got dark and Dr. Lombardi stood and began to talk. I was instantly captivated.[1]

Although three years have passed since that conference session, I can still see myself straining to hear every word, taking it in as I furiously jotted down notes. I felt like I had encountered the future, essentially walking through some kind of portal, leaving behind everything that I thought I knew about technology use in an educational setting and into something much broader and more meaningful, something more like an interactive treasure map for learning in the 21st century. Not only could Croquet bring educators out of their traditional mindset, it promised to totally blow their minds. I imagined teachers everywhere leaping out of their boxes, never returning to the ineffective practices that had marked some days in the classroom. For the first time, I knew what a religious convert in a charismatic cult felt like. I was smitten.

I kept sneaking glances around the room, wondering if everyone was as excited as I. A few others took notes, but most sat listening politely. I assumed they were overwhelmed and dumbfounded. I appeared to others, most likely, to be also sitting quietly, but in truth my mind was racing alongside the presenters, not only absorbing as much as I could about what the Croquet project was and what it might mean in the future, but also how I might harness the technology and put it to my own use, which was redesigning the traditional college history classroom with epistemic games at the core. I was ready to scrap everything I'd been doing and walk down this new path.

By the end of the hour I'd scribbled down a half-dozen possible ways in which I might use the Croquet software, and I'll admit that my grandest scheme would likely need to be accompanied by a budget that would light up faces in the military. Although Croquet is an open-sourced platform and network operating system, the likelihood that my PhD in American History and I could create what I was imagining was slim to none. I'd need an army of technical folks to help me develop a semester-long, collaborative, multi-user U.S. History survey game. But I knew, given the time and talent, such a use would be possible with Croquet.

I imagined college students engaging in a virtual past-world for sixteen weeks where some were English explorers, crossing the ocean only to encounter their peers who had begun the game as Narragansett. Decisions would be made by these "players" that might reflect the past or prove counter to it, but either proposition burst with promise. The students would be fully immersed in play that would evolve over time, and their characters would interact with the environment, their peers, a variety of primary sources, and events. I didn't know how this would work, but I imagined that the characters they began with would grow old and die and that the student would need to become a second character. The object, of course, was to move them through the major periods representing American history. They would relive the past, grow in empathy, grasp cause-and-effect, and subconsciously learn facts and chronology along the way.

As I walked out of the ballroom following the end of the session, I told myself that this massive, multi-player, online history "class" wasn't realistic immediately, but I would file it in my "someday maybe" folder and keep it in mind. My excitement made me more gregarious than usual, and I bounded up to my boss beaming. He had missed the session. I gushed, babbled, and flooded him with a host of ideas. He had been talking with a friend from another university and after introductions were made, my torrent continued to flow. The friend smiled and shook his head in agreement so I asked him what he'd thought of the session and of Croquet.

He looked around uncomfortably and quietly said, "I guess I could create a virtual classroom and have my students meet in it to hear me lecture."

I don't have much of a poker face, and I think that my jaw literally dropped. Here was this amazing opportunity to totally rethink educational environments and the ways in which people could learn in terms of space, content, interaction, and collaboration and it was now clear to me that many attendees hadn't gotten it. Those folks sitting there politely were just sitting politely. Their minds were not racing to see how this software or the ideas it introduced might inform or change their teaching practices. They had not walked through the portal. They were as firmly entrenched in their boxes as ever.

"Ah, a new technology," I imagined they thought. "Another passing fad to be avoided at all cost." I won't argue that many technologies and educational policies represent the current "hot" topics only to be forgotten when the next wave of new ideas or gizmos emerge. Croquet software may well be among those passing phases, but it was not the software platform or its creators that got me so excited that day at the conference: it was the promise and possibility that we were collectively thinking about better ways to engage students today and in the future.

Millenials

Much has been written about the Millennial Generation of students who are coming of age and entering colleges today. The tendency to understand people—and students by default—through a selection of aggregated characteristics has been in vogue for several decades and represents a simplistic means of profiling. Originally developed as a marketing and advertising tool, this group biographical sketch has been adopted by educational leaders as a call-to-arms in the effort to revitalize the college classroom.[2]

Educational leaders argue that today's college students are fundamentally different from those in the past and that teaching methods must adapt and change to meet the needs of these "new" students. Millennial students are defined as those born between roughly 1982 and 2000 and who have never known a world without personal computers and the internet. As a group, they are "digital natives"—comfortable with technology and largely products of its influence. They are confident, self-assured, have high self-esteem, and an optimistic outlook on life. In their working lives, they are ambitious and success and goal oriented. At the same time, they exhibit a collaborative team mentality and are strongly oriented toward their peers. Millennials prefer working and learning situations that depend on collaboration and group or team effort and evaluation over individual competition.[3]

In the book *Connecting to the Net Generation: What Higher Education Professionals Need to Know about Today's Students,* authors Reynol Junco and Jeanna Mastrodicasa conducted a survey of 7,705 college students in the United States and found that:
- 97 percent own a computer
- 94 percent own a cell phone
- 76 percent use Instant Messaging (IM)
- 15 percent of IM users are logged on 24 hours a day for 7 days a week
- 34 percent use websites as their primary source of news
- 28 percent author a blog and 44 percent read blogs
- 49 percent download music using peer-to-peer file sharing
- 75 percent of college students have a Facebook account
- 60 percent own some type of portable music and/or video device such as an iPod[4]

Such findings reinforce the theories about millenials and illuminate the practical, anecdotal evidence gathered by teachers.

Marc Prensky first articulated the "discontinuity" that emerged between today's student and the educational environment in which they were forced to "learn." Prensky argues that "today's students think and process information fundamentally differently from their predecessors" and that because of their life-experience, particularly the influence of technology, their brains have potentially "physically changed—and are different from ours."[5]

The "ours" he is referring to are the teachers, administrators, and academic leaders who establish the norms by which today's students learn, and he argues that the educational community "speaks an outdated language" and "struggles to teach a population that speaks an entirely new language." Prensky refers to today's students as Digital Natives and summarizes their learning styles. Digital Natives:
- Like to receive information quickly
- Like to parallel process and multi-task
- Like random access (hypertext)
- Like to network—are highly social
- Thrive on instant gratification and multiple rewards
- Prefer seeing graphics and images before encountering text
- Prefer games to "serious" work[6]

Many educators encountering Millennials feel frustrated. Pedagogical techniques that worked for a dozen years are no longer effective. Teachers complain about students' short attention spans or their unwillingness to read long novels like *Moby Dick*, or for that matter, to read multiple short novels. Are students' attention spans shorter than they used to be? Are today's students not interested in learning?

Prensky argues that the opposite is the case. Students are very interested in learning—just not in learning through the old methods. As quoted by Prensky, one high school student said that "every time I go to school I have to power down." Or as a former college student stated, "I went to a highly ranked college where all the professors came from MIT. But all they did was read from their textbooks. I quit."[7]

19th Century Learning

"Today's child is bewildered when he enters the 19th century environment that still characterizes the educational establishment where information is scarce, but ordered and structured by fragmented, classified patterns, subjects, and schedules." Scholar and philosopher Marshall McLuhan made this statement in 1967, but he could easily be describing today's classroom.[8]

By the early 1900s, most states required children to attend elementary schools, promising to offer every American a basic standard of learning in the areas deemed essential—math, reading, and civic awareness—and in specific American "virtues," in an attempt to assimilate the thousands of immigrants arriving from Southern and Eastern Europe. Teachers relied on two primary pedagogical methods: lecture and rote memorization, and these methods were used from the elementary through university classroom. The increasing urbanization and need for factory labor required by the economy demanded a work force that had a basic education, but that also respected authority and would tolerate repetitive tasks. The emerging educational system sought to train just such a labor pool and did it so effectively that the system of education devised is still in use today. How did schools reinforce the values desired in the work place?

Schools set regular hours and demanded student punctuality not just at the beginning and end of the day, but also throughout the day, regulating and dividing classroom content time into periods through the use of bells. Subject-matter was divided neatly into packages, and all students were expected to learn the same content in the same manner in the same amount of time. For example, the first hour of the day might be devoted to math. The teacher would instruct the students in the day's concept, the students would practice the concept by completing one or two worksheets, and then the bell would ring and the students would file out of the room and on to the next class where they would repeat the exercise with a different subject matter.

It mattered little if or how the concepts covered over the course of the day might relate to each other. Teachers did not attempt to teach across disciplines or make connections so students didn't bother to either. Did it matter if a student learned in English class that an acre was a unit usually associated with measuring land, even though one hour later in Math class, the same student was told that one acre equaled 4,480 square feet, which was smaller than a football field, and another hour after that in History class that settlers could apply for 160 acres under the Homestead Act in 1862? The same student might complete the day in Reading class reading one of Laura Ingalls Wilder's books learning that her family filed a homesteading claim on 160 acres in South Dakota. Would the student make the connections throughout the day that this small unit of measurement—the acre—could hold so much meaning, hope, fear, and promise?

Just as the elementary and secondary school system was broken into rigid segments, the collegiate educational experience underwent a similar standardization when the "Credit Hour" or "Carnegie Unit" became the primary means by which administrators could manage and compare students, faculty, and institutions. The credit hour has evolved as a time-based reference for measuring educational attainment, and student course work and degrees are determined by this unit measurement. Additionally, faculty workload and efficiency as well as budgetary and space allocations are dependent on the credit hour concept.[9]

As with the division of time and subject matter used in primary schools, the credit hour measurement is a false and arbitrary method developed more for its ease of management and bookkeeping than as an accurate reflection of student growth and learning. Despite the fact that it stands in stark contrasts to the research on how humans actually learn best.

During the same period that schools and colleges were becoming mini-factory systems, educator and reformer John Dewey was arguing for a system that took the complete opposite approach, a system that integrated learning with doing for the whole person. Dewey's philosophy on education emphasized the broadening of the intellect through problem solving and critical thinking. He argued that this could not be achieved through the memorization of facts. Although Dewey was well respected his ideas were not implemented widely at the time.[10]

But the ideas Dewey promoted have continued to garner interest and evolved into several different theories of learning, including those associated with constructivism, which views learning as a process in which the learner actively builds or scaffolds new ideas or concepts on top of knowledge acquired previously by solving realistic problems. Constructivists ask what good does it do for a student to memorize hoards of facts to pass a standardized test? Will the student remember it five years later? Two years later? The truth is that the majority of students won't remember the names or dates from their test only 24 hours later, and they certainly could never apply the knowledge that they had memorized and expunged for a test.

While rote memorization may have adequately prepared America's labor force for the factory floor, it cannot produce the kinds of workers needed in the 21st century. As James Paul Gee writes in the forward to *How Computer Games Help Children Learn*, "Young people today need to be able to use their learning muscles to innovate and create, and ultimately to adapt and transform themselves several times over in one lifetime. They need to be tech-savvy if they are going to have any hope of a secure future."[11] Today's students must be able to function in a rapidly changing world—they

must be able to think quickly, find reliable information in a wealth of disinformation, summarize efficiently, and then transmit their thoughts through various media outlets. The 19th century classroom is not teaching our children the skills they need to perform this task.

The 21st Century Classroom

What will the 21st century classroom look like? This question must be answered as a direct reflection of how the 21st century student will look and what their lives will be like. We know that foreign policies and the global economy are making the world "flatter" and creating industries reliant on a highly-skilled work force proficient in critical thinking skills and information literacy. As David Williamson Shaffer has argued, "the high end of the value chain in a global economy is the knowledge needed to design innovative products, services, and technologies that let people share information, work together, and do things in new ways." He claims, "in the very near future, the only good jobs left will be for people who can do innovative and creative work."[12]

If innovation and creation is the future, our current educational system is ill prepared. Attempting to "leave no child behind" may be a noble effort, but standardized tests and months of "drill and kill" will not teach our students to think and act critically. Today's students have become very good at "school." They have mastered the art of memorizing facts, regurgitating them on tests, and then forgetting them. We have trained them to be bulimic learners, but what use will this be to them when they need preparation in higher-order thinking?

The Humanities Classroom

Departments in the Humanities at colleges and universities often believe that they are bastions of critical thinking, assuming that engaging with the content of their disciplines will imbue students with the ability to think, write, and read critically. This attitude is mirrored in the ways in which academics define the humanities. Instead of relying on the typical definition of humanities as a group of academic disciplines that includes, for example, history, philosophy, literature, ethics, and art criticism, the Massachusetts Foundation for the Humanities argues that the humanities are a "way of thinking about and responding to the world—as tools we use to examine and make sense of the human experience in general and our individual experiences in particular" . . . enabling us to "reflect upon our lives and ask fundamental questions of value, purpose, and meaning in a rigorous and systematic way."[13] Defined this way, the word "humanities" could be used interchangeably with "critical thinking" or "higher-cognitive thinking."

Clearly this is not the case. We have all taken humanities classes that required little actual thought; the stereotypical example would be the history course taught by the school coach. Unfortunately even well meaning instructors who teach their content diligently and believe in the importance of critical thinking are often unaware that while they may talk about theory, evaluation, and synthesis in their lectures, their tests privilege recall. And most students learn to the test. So while an instructor might expect a student to walk out of their Intro to Philosophy course understanding that branches of philosophy exist as mirrors to a specific time, it is more likely that the student would have spent the semester making flash cards with the names of the major branches, plus a brief definition. This is not a matter of multiple-choice exams versus essay, either, as overwhelmingly students cram four times during a term, regardless of the test format, and assume after they turn it in that they are done with that information. Out it goes in favor of the newest, latest bits that they will be required to recall for the next exam.

Humanities' instructors cannot assume that talking about higher order thinking is enough either, especially when the talk is one-directional. Instructors must not only act as authority figures when it comes to their content, but they must also model directly and physically the kinds of thinking that they want their students to do. Most students need overt training to develop the skills necessary to both understand and evaluate subject matter. The National Commission on Excellence in Education in a landmark report written in 1983 stated, "many 17-year-olds do not possess the 'higher-order' intellectual skills we should expect of them. Nearly 40 percent cannot draw inferences from written material; only one-fifth can write a persuasive essay; and only one-third can solve a mathematics problem requiring several steps."[14]

To engage in the kind of modeling needed, instructors must move away from lecturing predominantly and find new ways to reach today's students. Raymond S. Nickerson, who is an authority on critical thinking, argues that people who think critically think not only with knowledge, but also with an attitude that they have cultivated over time. He says that critical thinkers:
- Suspend judgment when evidence to support a conclusion does not exist
- Understand the idea of degrees of belief
- See patterns that are not superficially apparent
- Organize thoughts and convey them concisely and coherently
- Learn independently and enjoy doing so
- Recognize that their own beliefs and opinions are fallible
- Transfer knowledge from one domain to another

Instructors must find ways to model the actions of critical thinkers in the classroom to grow the attitude of critical thought in their students. For the most part, our traditional college classes are having the exact opposite effect in students. The video Michael Wesch's students at Kansas State University made and posted on YouTube, "A Visions of Students Today," became a rallying cry from Millenials for the kind of learning they crave. Millions of students sent the link to their instructors, demanding that their needs be heard.[15] See the video at: http://www.youtube.com/watch?v=dGCJ46vyR9o

Next Generation Course Redesign™

The work in course redesign ongoing at the University of North Texas is grounded in the belief that we owe today's students an education that will provide for their future. The view of course redesign presented here grows out of the constructivist, epistemic tradition of the last century and is founded on the belief that student success is directly related to an education based on real-world, relevant, problem-based experiences taught through active learning pedagogies. We want our students to be prepared for life-long learning in a changing world. To achieve this goal, we have examined our current assumptions about teaching and redirected our effort away from ourselves as instructors and refocused it on our students. What or how we teach is no longer our primary concern. What and how students learn has become paramount.

The random boundaries that previously defined our classrooms are being knocked down. We have questioned the traditional system and discovered that we need not define our subjects by credit hours or false compartmentalization. We are confronting the old modes of knowledge and are creating new ones that are more porous and flexible.

We aim to transform our large courses from passive to active environments that encourage deep learning and thinking in an effort to teach to the future—with dynamic, engaging content, innovative pedagogies, and metacognitive frames. Each of the classes altered through the Next Generation Course Redesign™ Project looks different, informed by the discipline and by the community of practice of instructors generated by the project. Although the look and feel of the courses vary dramatically, each represents what the 21st century classroom will look like because each class meets certain basic conditions:
• Student learning is the focus
• Content is learned actively
• Problem-solving is a priority
• Collaboration is essential

The University of North Texas is mid-way through a multi-year project to redesign twenty-five of its core large enrollment courses. A two-year pilot project in blended learning preceded the N-Gen course redesign effort and the two combined will result in the redesign of a minimum of at least thirty-five classes. These courses represent the basic subjects that all students attending the University must take, and because they are required, they are traditionally taught in a large lecture format in 150, 300, or even 500 student sections.

Despite the best efforts of faculty, these courses consistently have high drop, fail, and withdrawal rates. UNT is not the only institution struggling to cope with large classes. A recent article in the Washington *Post* detailed the challenge faced by institutions across the nation as faculty struggle to effectively teach students in big classes. Dr. Carl Wieman, 2001 Nobel Prize winner and teaching-reform advocate, is quoted as saying that "In a very real way, you're doing damage with these courses." Wieman argues that students "tune out and are turned off" in the large lecture class. Students are not only NOT learning facts, but they are not learning the scientific approach to problem-solving. Wieman's own research has revealed that students taking his physics class in the large lecture format actually think *less* like professional physicists after course completion as compared with before they began the class. Wieman supports teaching pedagogies that enable students to learn material independently with only guidance and support from faculty. He says, "it's [active learning] not necessarily popular with students, but the cognitive research says it is the way to make learning stick."[16]

For students to learn effectively, institutions must support faculty in efforts to alter course pedagogy from solely lecture-based to more active learning/teaching strategies. This effort represents a huge challenge and requires faculty to think creatively about instructional delivery, particularly in the ways in which they might utilize technology. But the kind of changes called for by the 21st century classroom will likely counter most institution's cultural values and tenets. Kay M. McClenney, Vice President of the Education Commission of the States, summarized this problem in higher education, saying

> The reality is that innovation does not equal transformation, and multiple innovations do not add up to fundamental change. Effective innovations are seldom effectively replicated. Even when replicated, innovations seldom change institutions or systems. Evidence of this fact is widely available and equally widely ignored. It is convenient to ignore because otherwise we might have to disrupt the status quo. In fact, the willingness to allow innovation on the margins is a way of containing it, preventing it from contaminating "core functions." Innovation on the margins relieves pressure on the institution to create more essential change.[17]

Several universities have attempted course redesign but most efforts have resulted in isolated changes that do not diffuse throughout a single department, much less the entire institution.

The N-Gen Course Redesign process developed at UNT encourages transformative innovation that reaches to the core of learning. Both a process and a product, N-Gen Redesign reinvigorates instructors and students and brings passion back to the classroom. Today's 21st century students want to learn, and they are demanding that experts find ways to reach them and prepare them for the future. Course redesign focused on collaborative, constructivist-based pedagogies is ripe with the promise of engaging today's students and meeting their needs.

The Structure of This Book

This book is structured so that either an individual or a team of instructors can move through the process of course redesign developed by the N-Gen Course Redesign Project™. Faculty involved in this project at UNT spend a year as part of a community-of-practice that includes administrators, support staff, other faculty, and students. Each phase of the process corresponds with a chapter in this book, mimicking the method for instructors who wish to redesign their classes on their own or for faculty professional development staff that would like to lead a similar project on their own campuses.

Chapter One address the challenges faced by instructors teaching today's students and provides the underlying principles, practices, and research that inform N-Gen Course Redesign™. By the end of the chapter, an instructor will have written a Teaching Philosophy Statement and determined what they want their students to know and to be able to do and decided what kind of impact they want to have on their students long-term.

Chapter Two walks the instructor through a Course Needs Assessment and the creation of a Course Concept Map for significant learning. Chapter Three moves the instructor into the foundation of redesign—writing and validating Student Learning Outcomes (SLO). Chapter Four summarizes the need for outcomes based assessment and explains the links between SLOs, assessment, and student success. With measurable SLOs in place and a comprehensive assessment plan created, instructors will be ready to think about instructional activities, materials, and course structure, which is addressed in Chapter 5. Additionally the chapter addresses the need to use data collected form the course to make modifications and changes for the future.

Chapters Six through Nine are case studies of specific humanities courses redesigned at the University of North Texas using four different approaches. The classes illustrated are U.S. History I, Music Appreciation, Art History II, and World Literature I. The book concludes with a summary of the N-Gen redesign process and additional support materials available to help instructors and institutions as they move forward with transforming their classrooms for the 21st century.

C　H　A　P　T　E　R　　　　O　N　E

Why Course Redesign?

In 1985 the United States Congress charged the National Endowment for the Humanities and the National Endowment for the Arts to study the state of art and humanities education in the nation. A diverse advisory group, representing every geographical and socio-economic niche in the country, concluded that art, history, literature, and the languages are inadequately taught to America's youth. They determined that students do not have a basic knowledge of the facts, culture, or a shared knowledge of society. A nation-wide survey revealed that more than two-thirds of American 17-year-olds cannot place the Civil War in the correct half-century or identify the Reformation. These young adults do not know the major events, personalities, literature, geographical location, or art of our nation or the world.[1]

Few humanities teachers today would disagree with the results of this study. Instructors often decry the state of today's students, complaining that they are arriving at college not prepared for the work. Most, they argue, cannot write a paper or recall basic facts on a test. Teachers reminisce about the students of yesterday: how much more willing they were to work; how they came to class prepared and eagerly listened to every word of the lecture. In short, how much better students were in the past as compared with today.

Yet a study conducted in 1917, comparable with the one carried out by the NEH in 1987, revealed the same student characteristics. J. Carleton Bell and David McCollum tested 668 Texas high school students and published their findings in the *Journal of Educational Psychology*. The results differ little from subsequent similar surveys. In 1942 and again in 1976 the *New York Times* conducted surveys on American youth about History—both studies found high school students' knowledge severely limited.

The 1987 National Assessment of Educational Progress found students "at risk of being gravely handicapped by . . . ignorance upon entry into adulthood, citizenship, and parenthood."[2]

The public, reading the results from these and other surveys like them, have drawn conclusions much like those made by many of today's instructors: students don't know anything! Some blame the educational system, arguing that it values skills over knowledge. Others blame textbooks or content periodization. Some even venture into pedagogical approaches, arguing that one teaching method is superior, while others argue that no single pedagogy should ever dominate a classroom.

What seems clear from the conversations these studies have generated is that the public believes that students should have a working knowledge of our history, culture, and art. What is less clear and more troublesome is how teachers are to impart that knowledge. The public has been quick to complain, but reluctant to instigate the core changes needed to the educational system. Instituting a standardized test across the nation (such as No Child Left Behind) is a simple, quick "fix," but it ends up not being a fix at all, merely a bandage masking the fundamental changes needed.

And yet a call for such a fundamental change is coming from multiple directions. Several institutions have made the move toward becoming a "learning paradigm college." This term, coined by John Tagg, is used to contrast his vision of an educational ideal with the current system, a system he calls the "instructional paradigm college." Tagg began thinking about the fundamental changes needed in institutions, saying, "It seemed that the more seriously I took the task of teaching, the more difficult it became, and many of the difficulties seemed to be a product of the overall design of the system in which I worked." He and colleague Robert Barr began to clarify a theory based on their experiences and first published it in an article in *Change* magazine in 1995. Reaction was instantaneous—much positive, but also some vehemently negative.

Tagg believes, and data supports, that colleges and universities are not fulfilling their fundamental purpose and are not serving the needs of students or society. Although many institutional leaders agree, clear barriers exist to initiating purposeful reform in institutions as they now exist. False structures must be eliminated, particularly since students today are so radically different and have such different needs than those in the past.

The purposeful reform Tagg and others propose involves moving away from thinking about teaching to thinking about learning. The three-credit hour (Carnegie) system is an example of how institutions rely on a "teaching" paradigm instead of concentrating on learning. Dividing each class into 3 hour segments (or 4 hour, etc.) and total degree programs into 120, 133, or 145 hour requirements makes book-keeping simple. A student takes X number of classes at 3 hours a piece, resulting in 120 hours and voilà, they are done—graduated!

But few students learn every subject by spending 3 hours a week, 45 hours a semester, sitting in a classroom. For some, a class may be mostly a refresher of material they have learned previously. They would benefit far more by taking a shortened version, perhaps lasting only 8 weeks—instead of the typical 15—moving through the material at a much more rapid pace. The same student who flew through a basic math course might need more time to learn a foreign language and would benefit by having the course last 25 weeks. No two people learn the same material at the same rate of proficiency, and yet institutions have created artificial boundaries that assume all students do just that.

The institutionalization of learning, of which the Carnegie System is only one example, encourages students to take a surface approach to learning in general. Students are fully aware that it is their performance on tests that matter most in the majority of college classes, and they become proficient at memorizing and repeating the facts required for the exam.

John Bowden and Ference Marton in their book *The University of Learning* argue "One of the greatest problems in institutional forms of learning is that students study for the tests and exams, instead of studying to grasp the object of learning and instead of studying for life." The kind of learning focused on recall of vast amounts of information is most often associated with *surface learning*, or learning for the sake of reproduction. It is by its nature superficial and is in opposition to *deep learning*, which is learning for the sake of comprehending meaning.[3] As professor Paul Ramsden states in *Learning to Teach in Higher Education*, " . . . the outcomes of students' learning are associated with the approaches they use. *What* students learn is indeed closely associated with *how* they go about learning it."[4]

If we want students to learn, we must rethink not only our content choices but also our teaching approaches. We must move beyond the false institutional barriers that have been created to make accounting easier and begin to envision new ways in which to learn.

Learning Environments

The ways in which an environment is shaped can significantly influence the kinds of learning that will occur. Tagg argues that changes made in the individual classroom are not enough—reorganization at the highest levels of the institution are needed to move away from the Instructional Paradigm, and I agree. Many institutions are already moving in this direction and the recent emphasis from the United States Secretary of Education on learning accountability will push institutions further toward the Learning Paradigm. But just as change must be supported from the top, it must also be made at the grass-roots level. Instructors must make a commitment to designing their classes for deep learning.[5]

What is a college classroom? Most students enter college with a set notion of what a college classroom will be like. Their ideal is based on years of experience in the public school system, supplemented by Hollywood movies and conversations with their peers and parents. Students have formed a body of expectations of what the classroom environment will entail:

- Instructor as sole source of knowledge
- Lecture to convey content
- Textbook that is required by the instructor, but considered optional reading by the student
- Quizzes, tests, possibly some homework, depending on the subject
- Grades used to evaluate "learning"

For the most part, students have disconnected their real lives from the classroom. School is something they do so that they can get the _____(fill in the blank with job, house, car, boat, etc) that they really want. School is an end-to-a-means and not connected with their daily lives. Real-life and relevant are not a part of the body of expectations for the classroom, and yet we know that unless students integrate the things they learn into their lives, the learning that takes place will remain at the surface level.

One of our goals as instructors must be to create classes that favor authentic, relevant instruction that requires deep learning and to encourage our peers to do the same so that students are receiving the same message across a department and the institution: we must value holistic learning for the sake of learning; we must value process and quality over quantity; and we must offer support to each other as we engage in this journey. A student walking into your class should not arrive having already mastered your expectations. Rather, they should be challenged from the start to tackle the problems presented to them in thoughtful and provoking ways.

The poet Robert Frost taught for many years at Amherst College, as well as at other institutions, and he claimed to ". . . hate academic ways. I fight everything academic. Think of what time we waste in trying to learn academically—and what talent we staunch with academic teaching." Frost disliked rote [surface] learning and disagreed with the idea that content acquisition equaled knowledge. What mattered, he wrote in his journal, was that "students are made to think fresh and fine, to stand by themselves, to make a case."[6]

Frost seems to be making the case that the goal of a college education should entail more than just career preparation. It should engender life preparation and enable students to become lifelong learners. The learning environments that we create should interweave higher cognitive level skills like analysis and synthesis with discipline-specific content in ways that provoke students' interests. Learning should challenge the student to think in new ways about things they already know and assist them with scaffolding and integrating new content that they acquire. It should reveal unknown potential and provoke them to do more.

Creating learning environments that can do all this is a huge challenge and one that must be tackled from both ends: by administrators committed to breaking down the institutional barriers that so effectively mute real change, and by individual instructors willing to engage in a process of designing their classrooms for real and deep learning. N-Gen Course Redesign™ provides a framework for addressing this challenge.

Large Enrollment Lecture Classes

At most state universities, the learning environment for freshman and sophomore students takes place within the context of the large enrollment course. These classes serve as gateways for upper division study and many enroll 200, 500, or 700 students in a single course section. For example, a recent study at the University of California Berkeley revealed that "172 courses enrolled more than 200 students, representing three to four percent of all undergraduate primary courses." Berkeley concluded that "although the percentage of large-enrollment courses relative to the total number of courses offered is small, the impact on students, particularly first-time students, is significant." More than 98 percent of the entering freshman class and 72 percent of transfer students took at least one large-enrollment course, with the majority of freshman taking more than 4 courses in this format.[7]

Despite a growing body of research that indicates that active learning, collaboration, and frequent feedback result in the greatest gains in student learning, most large enrollment courses are lecture-centered, asking little of students in terms of engagement and relying heavily on memorization and recall as validation of "learning." The sheer size and anonymity of the large lecture class create problems that are in opposition to good learning environments and do not promote the kind of intellectual development and success most institutions expect at the collegiate level.

When asked about teaching students in the large enrollment class, most faculty concur on the kinds of challenges they encounter with students:
- Poor attendance
- Poor performance
- Inattention during class
- Little preparation
- Little motivation

Students list similar kinds of concerns when asked about the large-class environment. Most are dissatisfied with the quality of their learning experience and named the things that bothered them most:
- Little interaction with faculty
- Little structure in lectures
- Little contact with teaching assistants
- Few or no discussion sections
- Inadequate classroom facilities
- Lack of frequent feedback

In multiple studies, both faculty and students note the same kinds of challenges in the large enrollment class that lead to less learning. These include no individual accountability, highly impersonal, and a large number of distractions, but the single most often cited problem was the lack of instructor-to-student interaction. As Donald Wulff, Jody Nyquiest, and Robert Abbott concluded in a study on student perception of large enrollment classes, "foremost among the dimensions of large classes that hindered students' learning was the lack of instructor-student interaction with opportunities for questions and discussions."[8]

Joe Cuseo drew the same conclusions in a similar study. A professor of psychology at Marymount College in California, Cuseo argued that little interaction between students and instructor, both in the classroom and in feedback on classwork, reduced student learning, motivation, and satisfaction. Why was there little interaction? Cuseo contends that the heavy reliance on lecture with little student involvement or activity dictates the lack of contact between faculty and students.[9]

More than 80 percent of faculty in the United States rely on lecture as their primary instructional strategy. Studies on the efficacy of lecture have found that lecture is effective if the goal is to organize, integrate, and update reading materials, to demonstrate enthusiasm for the subject matter, to relate course-relevant personal experiences, or to provide a context for issues and ideas to be introduced in the readings. But if the instructors' goal is to foster long-term knowledge retention, engage students in higher-order thinking, model knowledge transfer to new situations, or motivate students, lecture is not effective.[10]

The lecture as an effective teaching method has been questioned for decades. As early as 1931 Hamilton Holt, president of Rollins College in Florida, shocked his peers at a conference when he claimed that he had learned "virtually nothing" while attending Yale and Columbia. Holt argued that lecture was "probably the worst scheme ever devised for imparting knowledge," claiming that it is a "mysterious process by means of which the contents of the professor's notebooks are transferred by means of the fountain pen to the pages of the student's notebook without passing through the mind of either." Holt believed that students learned best when allowed to make personal discoveries in collaboration with their peers.[11]

There are several reasons why lecture is not the most effective teaching strategy available to faculty. Students spend little time-on-task when the lecture format is used. Most are not fully attuned to the lecture, and they begin to disengage after the first ten minutes. Lion F. Gardiner, former co-coordinator of the teaching assistant training program at the Graduate School-Newark, found in a study on course content retention that students retained only 42 percent of a lecture immediately afterward and retention dropped by another 20 percent when assessed a week later. This study indicates that at best, students remember only 18 percent of the content spoken in a lecture class.[12]

Also, lecturers make assumptions about students that are not valid. These assumptions presume that students all learn best through auditory techniques, need the same kinds of material presented at the same pace and at the same time and without any two-way dialogue with the presenter, and that they possess the pre-requisite knowledge to be able to appropriately and accurately scaffold new knowledge.[13]

Additionally, a study by George Kuh, John H. Schuh, and Elizabeth H. Whitt found a "compact of disengagement" existed between faculty and students in a lecture classroom where a silent agreement existed of "you leave me alone and I will leave you alone." The anonymity inherent in large classes establishes this relationship and creates a sense of irresponsibility in students. They do not feel accountable in class, which is reflected in their poor attendance.[14]

Many faculty feel overwhelmed when confronted with the research on lecturing since this is how they have been teaching *and* this is how they were taught. Most instructors know empirically that many of their students are not learning as well as they should but they don't know what or how they can teach to better assist their students. If not lecture, then what?

Teaching Philosophy

In informal conversations with college faculty, I have found that most have a sense of why they got into teaching in the first place and many have found their experiences in the large lecture class at odds with their notion of teaching. Most teachers entered their fields with a love for their discipline and an excitement to transmit that passion to others, but have not thought systematically about their objectives as teachers.

Writing down a formal teaching philosophy statement provides instructors with the opportunity to think purposefully and with reflection about their conception of teaching and learning, how they teach, and why they teach the way they do.
What should a teaching philosophy statement include?
• What teaching and learning means to you
• A description of how you teach (what methods do you employ?)
• Examples of your teaching strategies (what do you do in the classroom?)
• Justification of why you teach the way you do

The statement takes time to write and may be written for a variety of audiences, including personal, search committee, or tenure portfolio. Regardless of the intended audience, every statement provides the instructor with an opportunity to understand and communicate teaching goals and to see how these goals correspond with their actions in the classroom. Reflecting on and writing a teaching philosophy provides a springboard for answering the question posed above—if not lecture, what?

To help jump-start your thinking, answer these questions:
1. What instructional strategies (teaching methods) do you use when you teach? (This might include lecture, small or large group discussion, collaborative teamwork, computer assisted instruction, demonstration, peer learning, mastery learning, problem-based learning, case-based learning, jigsaw learning)
2. What instructional strategies have you found effective?
3. How have you evaluated student learning in your courses (tests, quizzes, homework)?
4. On a scale of 1 to 10, how do you rank your knowledge of instructional strategies?

5. What do you see as the main purpose of University teaching?
6. From your perspective, what are the top three responsibilities of a college professor?
7. Of a college student?
8. What characterizes good teaching?
9. What are potential obstacles to good teaching?
10. During the time you have been teaching, have you made changes in the ways you teach or the materials you use to teach? Why?

Most teaching philosophy statements are 1 to 2 pages long. Your statement should reflect your personality and could take the form of a narrative, list, poem, or even a video. While there are no limits to the creativity of your presentation, all statements should illustrate self-reflective thought. While the statement is about your teaching, student learning should be the focus. There is no point in teaching unless students are learning.

Student learning must be the central focus of teaching and should figure prominently in your formal teaching philosophy statement. If improving student learning is the goal and that goal is not achievable based on the current instructional strategies that you use, then you are ready to begin thinking about how you can redesign your classes for greater student success.

N-Gen Course Redesign™

In some ways, calling the N-Gen process "course redesign" is a misnomer because most college faculty have not "designed" their courses in the first place. The majority of Humanities PhD's spend their doctoral years training to do research in their fields and receive little, if any, instruction in pedagogy. A few institutions offer one-semester courses in "teaching" as preparation for fellowships within the institution. These courses are meant to prepare the academic, in the short term, for standing in front of a group of freshman in an introductory course; in the long term, for a lifetime of teaching. Given these goals, the one-semester preparation course, which can range from 1 to 3 hours in length, seems woefully negligent.

The "teaching" course at many institutions consists of several elements deemed crucial to running an organized and efficient college classroom. The elements covered usually include:
• Writing a syllabus
• Practicing a lecture
• Writing multiple-choice questions
• Handling misbehaving students

There is a wealth of literature available to the new teacher in pedagogy and college instruction, but many "teaching" courses ignore this historiography. Faculty who want to expand the course to include more readings or multiple-semester trainings are often waylaid. "There is not time," they are told, "to expand on training in teaching. Research will be rewarded when the graduate student enters the market and goes up for tenure—not teaching." For a long time this was true and tenure policies rewarded research, particularly publication, and gave only a perfunctory nod to the classroom. But, like much in academia, this is changing. Teaching is taking on a more central role in the hiring and promotion process, especially as accrediting agencies are forcing institutions to become more accountable. For the first time, faculty are being asked to write and measure Student Learning Outcomes, a form of accountability unfamiliar to almost everyone in the Humanities.

For most faculty, thinking overtly about how they teach, why they teach the way they do, and what content they teach is a new act and, faced with such a large task, most do not know where to begin. In fact, the very act of questioning the way they have been teaching is often frightening. Most faculty teach the way they were taught and that means lecturing.

Lecturing seats the knowledge in the classroom in the instructor and clearly delineates a hierarchical structure. Knowledge transmission is a one-way process: from content expert to novice, and this is the instructional framework from which most faculty begin the redesign process.

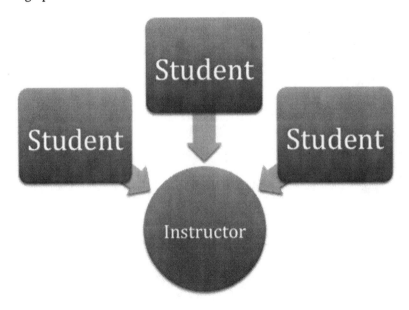

For some faculty, questioning the teaching process is synonymous with questioning their expertise, which can lead to something of an existential crisis. It isn't easy to let go of a preferred teaching style, even when intellectually it makes sense to do so. This process can take time and in many ways resembles the kind of thinking and learning that we want from our students. Just like students, instructors often have their own preconceived body of expectations when they think about what teaching in the classroom is like:

- Lecture
- Cover as much content as possible
- Test
- Focus on the instructor as the expert

Questioning one's teaching practices is difficult and involves a great deal of risk-taking. Deeply held ideals and values must be encountered head on and are sometimes found to be lacking. This kind of reflection may mean adjusting one's self-image, but it is an essential first-step in the redesign process.

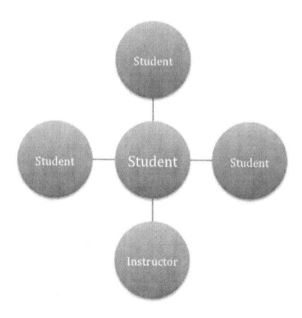

Square One Rethink

The N-Gen Course Redesign™ model begins by asking each instructor to question his or her role as a teacher, the role of the learner, and the role that education should play in students' lives. Because many of us are visual learners, I will also try to illustrate this questioning visually. I believe that instructors enter the classroom with a set of practices and expectations that they have built-up over a number of years. We will call this "in-the-box" teaching.

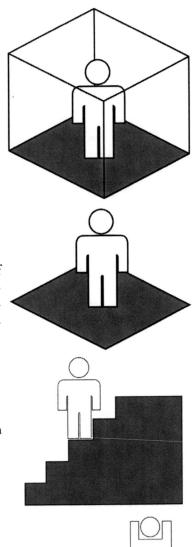

Step One:

The first step in the N-Gen process is to throw off the box and begin questioning the teaching practices in which we are engaged. This is the square-one rethink and it is from this ground-level exposure that new ways of learning will be born.

Step Two:

Stop concentrating on how you are going to teach and think instead of how your students can learn.

Step Three:

It's what students do that matters, and it is what they do that we will measure to determine whether they have learned.

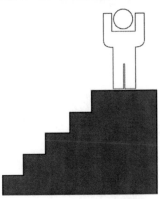

Once the instructor focuses on students learning, the box that was their teaching will have been transformed.

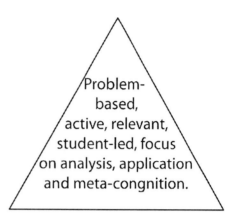

Lecture, passive, drill & practice, faculty-led, focus on memorization and recall.

Problem-based, active, relevant, student-led, focus on analysis, application and meta-congnition.

What is N-Gen Course Redesign?

Next Generation Course Redesign™ is built on a variety of course design models, pedagogical techniques, and assessment practices, taking the best theories and habits of each and combining them into a new strategy that results in powerful learning experiences. The process grows from a simple premise:

1. Higher cognitive-level Student Learning Outcomes (SLO) are desirable
2. Higher cognitive-level SLOs are achieved best through active learning
3. Active learning is facilitated best in small, collaborative groups
4. Small, collaborative groups can be achieved in the large-enrollment classroom by displacing some of the content of the "lecture," freeing time for active-learning and group activities

N-Gen Redesign emphasizes problem-solving, critical thinking skills, and valid assessments that can be generalized beyond a single class. The redesigns rely on experiential and problem-based learning pedagogies and high student engagement resulting in intrinsic motivation.

Designing the Learning Environment

L. Dee Fink, the founding director of the Instructional Development Program at the University of Oklahoma, has written extensively on course design, encouraging instructors to create courses that will result in significant learning experiences for students. In

his book *Creating Significant Learning Experiences in College Classrooms,* Fink defines significant learning as both a process and an outcome, arguing that "in a powerful learning experience, students will be engaged in their own learning, there will be a high energy level associated with it, and the whole process will have important outcomes or results." Fink ties the outcomes to change saying, "Not only will students be learning through out the course, by the end of the course they will clearly have changed in some important way." Fink believes that all significant learning offers at least one of the following:
- Enhancing our lives
- Enabling us to contribute to a group or our community
- Preparing us for work

Significant learning results in some fundamental change to the student that benefits him or her and society over a long period of time. Based on this definition, it seems impossible that surface learning would ever result in a significant learning experience.
- How do you begin creating significant learning experiences for your students? Pull out your teaching philosophy statement and, with it as a guide, answer these questions:
    1. What do you want your students to know and be able to do after taking your course?
    2. What kind of impact do you want to have on your students? In other words, ten years from now, what is the educational impact you want your teaching to have?

Do you want your students to be able to name 5 Renaissance paintings? Do you want them to know the date World War I ended? Perhaps you do because some foundational knowledge is a necessary component of being an educated individual, but these simple facts are not likely to be the impact that you want to have on your students in the long-term. My guess is that you wrote things like, "I want my students to be able to apply what they have learned in my class to their lives" or "I hope that my students will become critical thinkers, able to evaluate situations based on evidence."

Getting to that kind of higher-order thinking will require you to match your teaching goals and philosophy with instructional strategies that produce significant learning, regardless of whether you teach in a large enrollment format or not. Deciding how to do that in a way that is appropriate for your discipline and that matches your personal objectives forms the basis of the rest of this book.

After reading this Chapter, you should have . . .
1. a written statement of your Teaching Philosophy.
2. determined what it is that you want your students to know and be able to do after taking your course.
3. determined what kind of impact you want to have on your students long-term.

C H A P T E R   T W O

Making Best Decisions for your Discipline

Student James Webb slips into class a minute late. He's had car trouble, but managed to catch a ride to campus from one of his neighbors. There was no way he was missing class today—his small group is prepared to debate three other groups about the origins of Shakespeare's works. Was Shakespeare the author of the famous plays attributed to him or did someone else write them? James and his classmates have read a series of articles about the authorship controversy in preparation for the debate, and they still don't know which position they will be assigned to defend. He hopes they get to argue in favor of Christopher Marlowe. "What an amazing guy he was," says James to his group, "and to think—I didn't even know he existed before Dr. Gau's class."[1]

Professor Tracey Gau at the University of North Texas had taught a large enrollment class on Shakespeare for many years, and she had wanted her students to be more active in class. She felt like most of her time was spent reviewing plot, and she knew that wasn't what she really wanted to be doing with her students. She had always wanted her students to really get into the literature—"to own it"—but she didn't know how to get them that excited. Despite having taught the course for many years, she wasn't sure how to begin thinking about ways to change the course to achieve the objectives she'd established for herself in her teaching philosophy statement. To help kick-start the process, Dr. Gau completed a needs assessment for the course; the assessment helped her to troubleshoot areas in which her objectives were not aligned with her teaching strategies.

Course Needs Assessment

A needs assessment is a tool used most often in business for long-term planning. Instructional designers use it for a similar purpose because at its heart, it is simply a way to systematically explore the way things are as compared with the way you want them to be. A course needs assessment is the process of obtaining and analyzing information to determine the current status and needs for a particular course. Completing one for each of the courses you teach will help you to obtain information about the current conditions of the class as you now teach it, the problems or needs in the class, and the resources or approaches currently being used to approach the problems and needs.

A course needs assessment can be a powerful tool that will help you assign priorities and identify strategies to address them. I describe the process of conducting a course needs assessment below, and you will find a formal assessment following this section. Answer the questions posed and then hang on to your responses because we will return to the needs assessment many times in the next three chapters.

How To Do a Course Needs Assessment

The first step in performing a course needs assessment is to perform a "gap" analysis where you will determine what actually occurs in your class as compared with what you want to happen. The difference is the "gap" between your current and desired instruction. Defining this gap will assist you with identifying your needs, objectives, and purpose for this particular class.

This first step will produce a list of needs and challenges. Now compare this list with your teaching philosophy. How do they compare? What about a list of goals or objectives for your department or your institution? What are the realities and constraints under which you work in your department and institution that may influence the needs? Based on these comparisons, prioritize the needs and challenges you face in this class. If some of the needs are of low importance, or are unrealistic given the constraints you must work under, place them lower on the list of priorities and prepare to devote your energies to addressing the needs that are of higher importance.

Now you have a list of high importance needs and challenges that you are ready to address. These will be the areas in which you will focus your redesign efforts. You could begin brainstorming possible solutions, but for now, just hang onto the list. We will be pulling it back out again as we move through the rest of this book.

Course Needs Assessment

Course Title: _____

1. How many times have you taught this course?

2. How many students do you typically teach in this course? Is it a lower, upper, or graduate level course?

3. How often does the course meet? How long do class meetings last?

4. What are the physical elements of the course environment? How do they impact the class?

5. In the past, how have you determined what content will be taught in the course?

6. What are the curriculum expectations for this course? Do you determine them or are they determined by the college, department, or a professional society?

7. Is the course content primarily practical or is it theoretical? Is the field undergoing dramatic change?

8. In the past, what has been the primary method of instruction in this course? Why have you used this method?

9. In the past, have you used collaborative (group or team) teaching strategies in this course? What was the result?

10. In the past, have you attempted discussions or debates in this class? What was the result?

11. In the past, how have you evaluated student learning in this course? (For example, exams, quizzes, case studies, homework).

12. What are the characteristics of your students? What prior knowledge, experience, and feelings do they have about your field?

13. What are the preferred learning styles of your students? What is your preferred learning/teaching style? Does your learning style conflict with that of your students?

14. In order of importance, what do you expect students to know after taking this course?

15. In order of importance, what do you expect students to be able to do after taking this course?

Course Concept Map

Now that you have a prioritized list of needs/challenges for the course that you want to redesign, it's time to think about content. Look at questions five and six on the course needs assessment you just completed:

1. In the past, how have you determined what content will be taught in the course?
2. What are the curriculum expectations for this course? Do you determine them or are they determined by the college, department, or a professional society?

If you are like most humanities instructors, you determined what content you would teach in the course in two ways: thinking back to the content that you were taught when you took this class as an undergraduate or graduate student and by looking at the index in the textbook you plan to use. While these may be good starting points, they do not lead to good instructional strategies.

How can you determine what content will be taught that is more in line with your teaching goals? Even if some of your content is pre-determined by professional societies, your department, or your discipline's culture, you will still need to make decisions about what you will teach and what will be left out.

Most instructors know what they want to teach in a class—everything! But the truth is that you have only a limited amount of time and that means that you are going to have to make some hard decisions about what content you are going to deliver. Lecture may have been your primary instructional strategy in the past because you believed that it was the best way for you to "cover" all the material. Many instructors argue that they can *only* lecture because there isn't time to do anything else. They'd like for their students to explore a topic deeply, but if they take time out for that, they won't be able to "cover" all the material.

Recent research into student achievement in large-enrollment courses has thrown into question assumptions about the value of content coverage, suggesting that when it comes to student learning—*less is more!* For example, a study at the University of Akron revealed that when an instructor decreased content coverage in favor of inquiry-based, active learning in-class group problem solving, the students outperformed their peers who were enrolled in a traditional lecture course. The performance difference between the groups of students was even more dramatic on short-answer interpretation questions that involved synthesis, evaluation, and interpretation (those higher-cognitive level skills we want students to acquire). Students scored an average of 7 percent higher in the inquiry-based classroom, despite the fact that they had actually been directly exposed to *less* content.[2]

Marshall Sundberg, Michael Dini, and E. Li revealed similar findings in a study on freshman Biology for non-majors. They found that when content coverage was decreased and active-learning increased, both achievement scores and attitudes to science improved, as compared with classes where content coverage was stressed at the expense of context and participation.[3] Based on this research and that presented in Chapter One (students remember only 18 percent of a lecture), are we doing our students justice by insisting that we will "cover" everything there is to know about a topic?

Perhaps a better approach to determining what content to include is to think in terms of student learning. Given all the content there is in the course, what is (are) the most important things my students should learn? Educational consultants Jay McTighe and Grant Wiggins have developed a model of course design that promotes "teaching for understanding." They argue that teaching for understanding means that "students have something more than just textbook knowledge and skill—that a student really 'gets it.' Understanding then," they argue, "involves sophisticated insights and abilities, reflected in varied performances and contexts."[4]

McTighe and Wiggins suggest that instructors prioritize the concepts in their course into one of three buckets:
- "Enduring understandings"
- "Important knowledge and skills"
- "Worth being familiar with"

Concepts that are "enduring" are the ones held in high regard within the field. These have endured over time and are essential to know to understand the discipline. These are the concepts (theories, ideas) that students should retain years after the course is over.

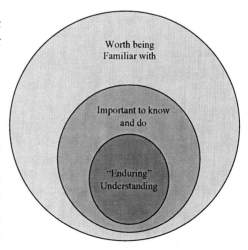

Adapted from Grant Wiggins and Jay McTighe, *Understanding by Design* (New Jersey: Merrill Prentice Hall, 1998), 15.

Keep these questions in mind as you begin to prioritize your course material:
1. To what extent does the topic, idea, or process represent a "big idea" in the field?
2. Is this big idea at the core of the discipline?
3. Can this big idea be "covered" or will it require that students explore it in-depth to understand it?
4. Will this big idea engage students?[v]

There are likely to be many topics and concepts that are valuable and interesting but they will not all require equal coverage nor may they all need to be covered in class, especially given the time frame in which you have to teach.

Keeping the "buckets" of curricular priorities in mind, begin creating your course concept map. A course concept map is a visual representation of the key concepts and ideas, the relationship between those concepts, and the course as a whole. In this instance, a concept is defined as a unit of thought or an element of knowledge under which experiences can be organized. Remember that the process of developing the concept map may prove more beneficial than the actual map. Ready to get started?
1. On a sheet of paper, write down key words for all the concepts that are important in the course.
2. Reduce this number by reading through the list of concepts. Eliminate concepts that are not that important (do not represent "enduring understanding") and combine concepts that are repetitive.
3. Write the concepts that remain on note cards or sticky note pads.
4. Sort the note cards into clusters
5. Label each cluster
6. Arrange the labels in a way that is meaningful
7. Transfer the cluster labels to a new sheet of paper and associate the sub-concepts with the primary label

Your goal in this exercise is to move away from thinking about your content as a list of lecture topics or chapters in a textbook to thinking about the course content as a whole. How can the material be integrated into one piece? There is no single right look or feel for a concept map—create whatever is most useful for your personality and the course subject matter. See below for examples of course concept maps for U.S. History.

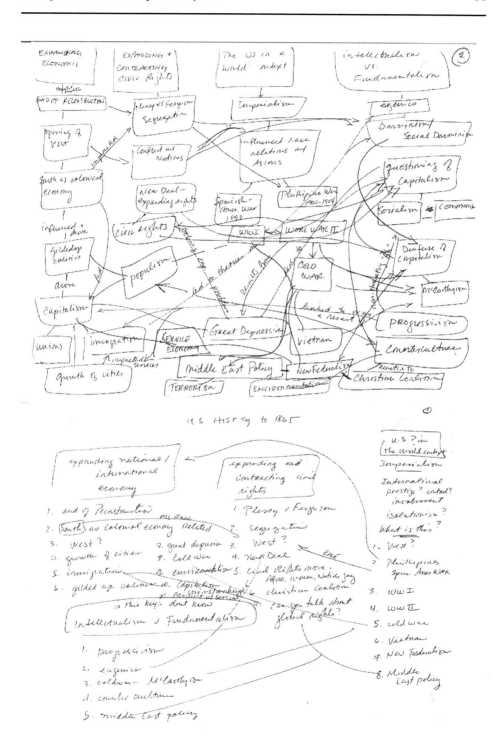

Significant Learning

Like the McTighe and Wiggin's ideas on "enduring learning," following L. Dee Fink's theories on significant learning will help you as you attempt to reduce or eliminate concepts that are interesting, but that do not form part of the core knowledge needed for the discipline. Fink has developed a "taxonomy of significant learning" based loosely on Benjamin Bloom's levels of intellectual behavior. Fink argues that the taxonomy of significant learning is interactive, meaning that each kind of learning listed can stimulate other kinds of learning. As you are thinking about the key concepts of your course, keep in mind the kinds of learning that your students will find significant.

Taxonomy of Significant Learning
1. **Foundational Knowledge**: learning at the level of understanding and remembering. This includes basic facts, chronology, terms, concepts, and principles.
2. **Application**: learning at the level of thinking in terms of critical, creative, or practical. This will include problem-solving and decision-making and the management of projects.
3. **Integration**: learning at the level of making connections such as finding similarities or differences.
4. **Human Dimensions**: learning at the level of changing oneself or being able to understand and interact with others.
5. **Caring**: learning at the level of identifying or changing one's feelings, interests, and values
6. **Learning how to Learn**: learning at the level of becoming a self-directed learner and learning how to ask and answer questions.[6]

Continue refining your course concept map until you feel that you have a clear visual representation of the core concepts and ideas and the relationships between those concepts. The concept map will serve as a starting point as you move into the next phase of course redesign: writing student learning outcomes.

Now that you have in mind the "enduring" principles of your discipline, you are prepared to think about the actions your students will take to make significant learning happen. Think of this as an iterative process that begins with creating measurable student learning outcomes that will be used to assess student learning. The outcomes and assessments will drive the course structure and the teaching activities. As you deliver the course and collect data, you will revisit the student learning outcomes, assessments, and teaching activities. Course redesign is an ongoing process as you learn to use data to drive your instructional decisions.

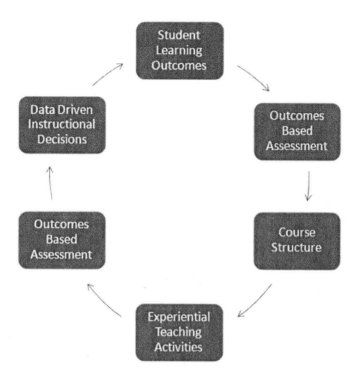

After reading this Chapter, you should have . . .
1. a completed Course Needs Assessment.
2. a completed draft of a Course Concept Map.

C H A P T E R   T H R E E

Start with the Student Learning Outcomes

Now that you have a clear idea of what the core concepts are for the course you are redesigning, you are ready to begin linking those concepts to student learning. You will develop your student learning outcomes (SLO) directly from your course concept map.

What are Student Learning Outcomes? Learning outcomes are descriptions of the measurable behaviors and products that you expect from students as a result of your instruction and their learning. In other words, learning outcomes are what students *are expected to be able to do* after being taught. Instructors match learning outcomes with assessments so that student learning can be measured. Once measured, instructors can make meaningful decisions about the kinds of learning that have occurred and adjust teaching practices, if needed. Why are learning outcomes important? Outcomes will help you to keep your focus on student learning!

All learning outcomes should:
- Focus on student learning
- Describe the students' expected behavior or product
- Set the conditions for the performance or behavior
- Be measurable
- Be clear and concise

How do I create and write learning outcomes for my students?

Writing learning outcomes is not difficult once you learn the basic idea:
 1. begin with a time limit in mind (like a semester, unit, or lesson)

2. then say "students will be able to . . ."
3. then use an action verb that describes the expected behavior or performance
4. then set any conditions, such as the situation or tools needed to perform the action

Here's an example of what I mean from a Japanese language class:

> *"By the end of the unit on food and culture, students will be able to recall in Japanese the names of the 15 fundamental foods that comprise the traditional Japanese diet."*

The instructor who developed this learning outcome expects the student to be able to recall basic information, a lower-level cognitive task. Faculty who want to have students engage in more than rote memorization can write learning outcomes aimed at higher cognitive tasks. For example, this learning outcome could be rewritten, requiring the student to engage in synthesis, a higher order cognitive skill:

> *"By the end of the unit on food and culture, students will demonstrate the ability to develop a menu in Japanese that features the majority of the foods that comprise the traditional Japanese diet."*

<u>The foremost thing to keep in mind is that Student Learning Outcomes are about Students Learning!</u>

Writing Higher-Cognitive Level Learning Outcomes

Now that you have some sense of what a student learning outcome is, you are ready think about writing SLOs at differing cognitive levels. Educators and psychologists have developed learning taxonomies that list the different types of learning that can occur and have arranged the learning types in a hierarchy. Researchers have identified three basic domains of learning: cognitive, affective, and psychomotor.[1]

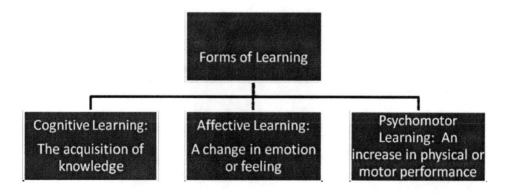

Learning Outcomes can be written for each type of learning (cognitive, affective, and psychomotor) and for varying levels within each type. Most courses designed for learning in higher education will emphasize cognitive learning. Bloom, Gagné, and Eisner have developed different taxonomies for learning in the cognitive realm.

Bloom's Taxonomy of Learning

In 1956, Benjamin Bloom published *Taxonomy of Objectives for the Cognitive Domain*. It has since become the primary taxonomy instructors reference in writing learning outcomes.[2] Bloom argues that there are six levels of cognitive learning:

1. basic knowledge
2. comprehension
3. application
4. analysis
5. synthesis
6. evaluation

Basic knowledge represents the most simplistic form of cognition and more sophisticated learning behaviors result from moving down the list, ending with evaluation. These six categories suggest specific kinds of behaviors that can be observed and measured to prove mastery of differing degrees of cognitive learning.

Keep in mind that tasks can vary on the taxonomy chart, depending on who is performing the task and how often it has been repeated. For example, a SLO such as:

"At the end of the lesson, the student will be able to tie their shoelace," might represent a high-cognitive level performance for a four-year-old who has never tied his shoelaces, but would fall much lower on the spectrum for a twelve-year-old who has already mastered this task.

Bloom Revision

In 2001, one of Bloom's students, Lorin Anderson, revised Bloom's original taxonomy, combining the cognitive process and the knowledge domain, making it easier for an instructor to align learning outcomes with assessment. In addition to modifying the names of the categories to reflect the active nature of thinking, the structure of the taxonomy changed to reflect a more useable view of both the knowledge to be learned (the knowledge dimension) and the process used to learn (cognition), making the taxonomy two dimensional.

Summary of Structural Changes from the Original Framework to the Revision

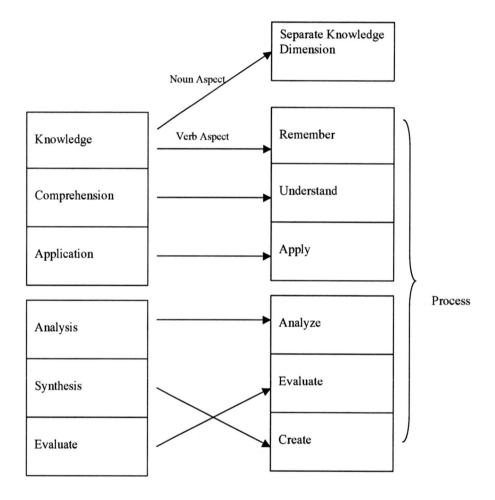

Lorin W. Anderson, "Taxonomy Academy Handbook," March 2005. The Anderson Research Group. http://www.andersonresearchgroup.com/tax.html Retrieved August 30, 2006.

Anderson constructed a Taxonomy Table representing the two dimensions with knowledge forming the vertical axis and the cognitive process forming the horizontal. The intersecting points of these two dimensions on the table form cells. Instructors can place their learning outcomes in the appropriate cell, allowing for a visual "check" on the degree to which complex kinds of knowledge and cognitive processes are being addressed.[3] See a version of Anderson's Taxonomy Table below.

The Revised Taxonomy for Educational Objectives

Knowledge Dimension	The Cognitive Process Dimension					
	Remembering	Understanding	Applying	Analyzing	Evaluating	Creating
Factual Knowledge						
Conceptual Knowledge						
Procedural Knowledge						
Meta-cognitive Knowledge						

To make writing learning outcomes easier for the instructor, Anderson and others have identified key verbs that can represent the cognitive processes.

Verbs for Writing Learning Outcomes

Remembering

Acquire	Distinguish	Name	Recognize	State
Cite	Draw	Quote	Record	Tabulate
Count	Identify	Read	Relate	Tell
Define	Indicate	Recall	Repeat	Trace
Describe	List	Recite	Select	Write

Understanding

Abstract	Compute	Differentiate	Express	Report
Associate	Convert	Discuss	Extrapolate	Restate
Classify	Contrast	Distinguish	Interpolate	Review
Compare	Describe	Estimate	Interpret	Transform
		Explain	Locate	Translate
			Predict	

Applying

Apply	Employ	Locate	Prepare	Sequence
Calculate	Examine	Operate	Relate	Schedule
Carry out	Explain	Order	Repair	Sketch
Complete	Generalize	Plan	Report	Solve
Demonstrate	Illustrate	Practice	Restate	Translate
Dramatize	Interpolate	Predict	Review	Use
	Interpret			Utilize

Analyzing

Analyze	Distinguish	Distinguish	Inventory
Appraise	Debate	Estimate	Question
Contract	Detect	Experiment	Recognize
Classify	Diagram	Infer	Separate
Criticize	Differentiate	Inspect	Summarize

Evaluating

Arrange	Compose	Formulate	Plan	Specify
Assess	Construct	Generalize	Prepare	Systematize
Build	Create	Integrate	Prescribe	Write
Collect	Design	Manage	Produce	
	Detect	Organize	Propose	

Creating

Appraise	Determine	Measure	Score
Asses	Estimate	Rank	Select
Check	Evaluate	Rate	Test
Choose	Grade	Recommend	Verify
Critique	Judge	Revise	

Example of SLOs Using Anderson's Taxonomy

Let's practice using Anderson's Taxonomy of Educational Objectives with the two learning outcomes we looked at in the early part of the chapter from the Japanese language class:

Knowledge Dimension	The Cognitive Process Dimension					
	Remembering	Understanding	Applying	Analyzing	Evaluating	Creating
Factual Knowledge	*By the end of the unit on food and culture, students will be able to recall in Japanese the names of the 15 fundamental foods that comprise the traditional Japanese diet*					
Conceptual Knowledge			*By the end of the unit on food and culture, students will demonstrate the ability to develop a menu in Japanese that features the majority of the foods that comprise the traditional Japanese diet*			
Procedural Knowledge						
Meta-cognitive Knowledge						

I have placed the learning outcomes within appropriate boxes, based on both the knowledge and cognitive process dimensions. Now I can visually see my outcome in a two-dimensional plane

Gagné's Taxonomy of Learning

Robert Gagné classified learning into five kinds of learning capabilities: intellectual skills, cognitive strategies, verbal information, attitudes, and motor skills.[4]
Being familiar with these capabilities will help you to further refine your SLOs.

Gagné's Taxonomy
Verbal Information   Memorization

Intellectual Skills
Applying
Knowledge   • Discrimination: the recognition of differing classifications
                • Concrete concept: classifying by physical features
                • Defined concept: classifying by abstract features
                • Rules: using a simple procedure to solve a problem
                • Higher-order rule: using a complex procedure to solve a problem

Cognitive Strategies   Using a process to solve a problem or accomplish a task
Attitudes   Behaving in a manner that illustrates a new value or belief
Motor Skills   Performing a physical task to a set standard

Of these five categories of learning, the category *"Intellectual skills"* has garnered the most attention. Within it, five hierarchical levels exist, each necessary to demonstrate mastery of a task. These levels build from the novice to the expert. Gagné argued that instructors must create learning hierarchies for the knowledge they expect students to acquire. A learning hierarchy is created by working backward from the final learning outcome, breaking the statement down to the varying skills needed for it to be accomplished. For example, working from our higher-cognitive level learning outcome:

> *"By the end of the unit on food and culture, students will demonstrate the ability to develop a menu in Japanese that features the majority of the foods that comprise the traditional Japanese diet."*

The instructor would determine the component skills needed for students to develop such a menu. This might include tasks such as:

- identifying the correctly translated words for the major traditional foods
- recalling the proper food combinations, particularly if the meal is part of a ceremony
- understanding the cultural norms and expectations the Japanese have imbued in their meal-taking

The instructor would analyze these component skills and arrange them in a hierarchy, breaking them down further, potentially, into even more basic skills. Following Gagné's taxonomy allows for a hierarchy of the learning activities needed to master the learning outcome. The skills formulated in the breakdown serve as prompts that support the learning process.

Six Facets of Understanding

Education consultants Jay McTighe and Grant Wiggins draw a distinction between what students "know" and what they "understand" that will help you to set curricular priorities and write SLOs. They argue that when a student truly understands the course material, he or she can demonstrate that understanding through at least one of the six facets of understanding. These facets are similar to Bloom's original taxonomy, but begin to point toward ways in which instructors can measure learning:

1. Explain: provide a thorough, supported, and justified account with supporting facts and data.
2. Apply: effectively use and adapt the information. Transfer the knowledge to a new and unrelated situation.
3. Interpret: tell meaningful stories, apt translations, provide a personal anecdote that relates to the idea, or make the material personal or accessible through models, images, or analogies.
4. Empathize: identify with a person, event, or idea that others might find odd, alien, or implausible.
5. Have Perspective: grasp points of view critically and objectively. See the "big picture."
6. Have Self-knowledge: perceive their own prejudices, projections, and habits of mind that impede their understanding. Aware of what they don't understand.[5]

Eisner's Expressive Models of Learning Outcomes

Elliot Eisner published *The Art of Educational Evaluation* in 1985, arguing that the learning *process* was just as important to measure and define as were the learning *results*. (So far, we've only been talking about the results of learning—not the actual process of learning). "Expressive" outcomes (such as you might want to use in performance art, theater, or dance) describe learning encounters, which define the situation, problem, or task, but not what specifically the student should learn from a learning experience. Creating "expressive" outcomes, Eisner argues, allows both the student and teacher the opportunity to explore his or her own interests within the defined outcome. In other words, the "expressive outcome" is evocative rather than prescriptive. Using expressive models alongside product-oriented outcomes could offer an instructor a broad snapshot of student learning.[vi]

How a Course Concept Map Relates to Student Learning Outcomes

You're now ready to begin writing your Student Learning Outcomes. Get started by pulling out your course concept map. Pick one of your main concepts. For example, using the U.S. History II concept map shown in Chapter Two, one of the big concepts is the idea of the U.S. in a world context. That's a major concept that I want to stress to my students, but that isn't a measurable outcome as it now stands. However, I can look down the list of items below it that fall under that core concept and find an event that serves as an example of that big concept. I know that I want my students to understand American Expansionism (Imperialism) and its long-term effects, and I know that I will use the Spanish-American War as an example of expansion. My outcomes associated with the idea of expansion might look like:

> Goal: The student will understand United States foreign policy after the Civil War.
>
> Objective 1: The student understands the roots and development of American expansionism and the causes and outcomes of the Spanish-American War by
> >   Outcome 1: tracing the acquisition of new territories.
> >   Outcome 2: describing how geopolitics, economic interests, racial ideology, missionary zeal, nationalism, and domestic tensions combined to create an expansionist foreign policy.
> >   Outcome 3: evaluating the causes, objectives, character, and outcome of the Spanish-American War.
> >   Outcome 4: explaining the causes and consequences of the Filipino insurrection.

I have used my course concept map as a spring board for writing my Student Learning Outcomes.

Now take your course concept map and do the same. Are the big concepts you want to teach equivalent to goals? Are they measurable? If not, can you break the concept into measurable pieces (as Gagné suggested)? Refer to Anderson's list of verbs to help you write your outcomes to varying cognitive levels, placing them on his two-dimensional taxonomy.

Why Write Learning Outcomes for My Class?

Writing learning outcomes for your course allows you to make your learning expectations clear to the student. It lets you develop outcome statements that are measurable so you can evaluate student performance continually and adjust teaching to improve student learning. The diagram below shows how outcome statements fit into an academic achievement model in which there is a symbiotic relationship between your learning outcomes, assessments that measure the outcomes, and instructional strategies that provide the opportunities for student learning.

See the individual course case studies in Chapters Six through Nine for specific examples of Student Learning Outcomes written by faculty who have been involved in the N-Gen Course Redesign Project™ at the University of North Texas.

Academic Achievement Model

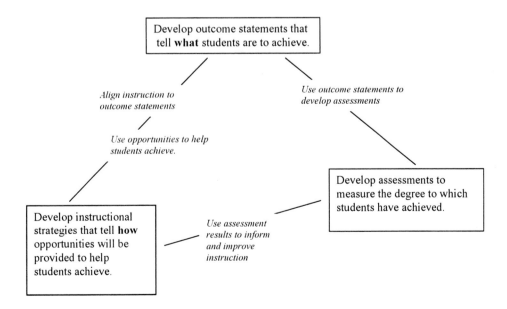

After reading this Chapter, you should have . . .

1.   written the Student Learning Outcomes for your course.

C   H   A   P   T   E   R   F   O   U   R

Outcomes Based Assessment that Leads to Data Driven Instructional Decisions

How do you know if your students have learned anything in your class? When posed this question, some instructors realize that they have not thought deeply about whether or not they have actually measured student learning. Most cite student grades, participation, or attendance, but realize fairly quickly that these are at best anecdotal indications of learning. Did a student learn the material in class or did they come in with pre-existing knowledge? How effective were specific teaching strategies in assisting students to learn the material? Did students actually learn what the instructor wanted them to learn? You cannot know this as an instructor unless you assess your students in a systematic way by linking your student learning outcomes with your assessments and your teaching strategies.

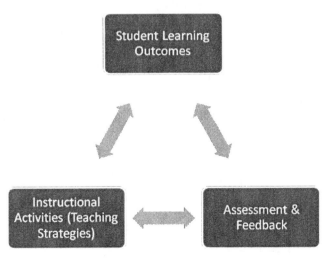

Recent studies indicate that student learning is declining at colleges in the United States, citing causation variables as wide-ranging as graduation rates and time-to-degree to learning outcomes and core literacy skills. For example, the most recent National Assessment of Adult Literacy found that the percentage of college graduates proficient in prose literacy had declined from 40 to 31 percent in the last ten years.[1]

Employers have noted the shortcomings in America's college graduates, claiming that recent hires are not prepared for today's work-world. They do not have the communication skills needed, and they cannot think and write critically, or effectively solve workplace problems.

In 2006 the Secretary of Education formed a commission to "chart the future of U.S. Education." The committee made several findings across key areas, one of which is accountability. Increasingly, accrediting boards are requiring institutions and departments to measure their programs in hard, quantifiable ways, and the only way to do this is through the use of established, common Student Learning Outcomes (SLO) linked with assessments that measure those outcomes. As we have already established in Chapter Three, SLOs ask us what it is that we expect students to be able to do and think once they have completed our course. The next step in this process is providing the evidence (measuring the learning) that proves what students have done and thought.[2]

Assessment may represent an entirely new way of thinking about student learning and the teaching experience for instructors, but it is one that students have always considered paramount. We have all experienced that moment during class when we are deep into an explanation about an important theory in our discipline when a student interrupts us to ask, "will this be on the test?" For students, assessment is of the uppermost importance. It defines for them how they will approach the course content, how they will study, and how much "work" they need to put into "learning" the material. Research indicates that students put in less than 10 percent of their time on material that is not assessed. "Assessment defines what students regard as important, how they spend their time, and how they come to see themselves as students and then as graduates." Students will look to the assessments to determine what is important.[3]

Assessment in the "Teaching Paradigm" Classroom

In the traditional classroom where teaching is the focus, students receive feedback most often through sporadic, high-stake exams. Most humanities instructors assess students three or four times during a semester by giving non-comprehensive tests. Assessment in this format "tells" the student that they have completed one hurdle in the syllabus and that they are ready to tackle the next in the slow-trudge toward the end of the class. Without even being aware of it, instructors are encouraging students to be bulimic learners—memorize everything for this one test, expunge it on the exam, and then never think of it again.

In addition to creating an anti-intellectual environment, this kind of assessment does not tell us anything about whether a student can put the knowledge they have acquired to use. High-stakes exams may weed out good test-takers from poor ones and assist teachers with a basis on which to award a grade, but these kinds of exams cannot determine whether a student is capable of using information acquired in a variety of unfamiliar and ambiguous real-world settings. If high-stakes exams cannot tell us this, then what kind of assessments would help us to determine true and authentic learning?[4]

Assessment in the "Learning Paradigm" Classroom

Scientists that study learning argue that it is a fairly simple exercise to test for subject matter recall, but it is much more difficult to measure a student's critical thinking, creativity, and problem-solving skills—yet these are the very characteristics that most institutions claim that they want to foster in students. To help students succeed with mastering these skills, instructors must move away from traditional forms of assessment and create assessments that are formative and developmental.

L. Dee Fink has written extensively on the differences between the traditional kinds of assessment that instructors use in the college classroom (he refers to this as "Audit-ive Assessment") as compared with the kinds of assessment that foster student learning and success (referred to as "Educative Assessment").[5]

In Audit-ive Assessment, instructors assess to assign a grade. All assessment is done at the end of learning (end of a lesson, unit, or the semester) to determine whether students understood the material or not.

Educative Assessment consists of four different kinds of assessment activities that help students realize whether they have learned correctly, but also assists them in learning *how* to learn. The four kinds of educative assessment include:

- Forward-looking assessment: includes activities, problems, and questions that mimic or create real-life contexts for a problem, issue, or decision that must be discussed and reached.
- Self-assessment: assists students with learning how to assess their own performances.

- Criteria and Standards: assists students with generating appropriate ways to evaluate their own work.
- "FIDeLity" feedback: includes feedback from instructor to student that is Frequent, Immediate, Discriminating, and Loving.
  - Frequent: given to students daily, weekly, or at the least, as frequently as possible.
  - Immediate: given to students as soon as possible.
  - Discriminating: evaluation based on clear criteria that differentiates between poor, acceptable, and exceptional work.
  - Loving: evaluations empathetically delivered.

Educative assessment is a process that involves both the instructor and the students in an integrated dynamic. The instructor is no longer the judge and jury in the classroom, but rather a co-creator with the students in a learning environment.[6]

What Counts as Evidence of Learning?

Instructors tend to rely on only one or two methods of assessment, most of which are chosen because the delivery is easy and the grading is fast. For example, an Art History instructor might give three multiple-choice tests during a semester delivered via Scantron. Apart from the time it takes to pass out the exams, the delivery process is easy and the grading even more so since the Scantrons are run through a machine. This kind of grading is summative, given at the end of a unit and the student has no opportunity to learn from or alter mistakes recorded.

Research tells us that while there is a place for summative evaluation, if we care about learning and having students learn for significant and enduring understanding, then we must use a variety of assessment methods in the classroom, including those most vital to the learning process—ongoing formative and informal self-assessments.

There are three main kinds of assessment:
- **Summative:** generally carried out at the end of a lesson, unit, or course. Used to complete a study and assign a grade.
- **Formative:** ongoing during a course of study. Primarily used as a learning tool to indicate mastery of content. Combined with additional work to aid the student in correcting mistakes and clarifying misconceptions. Is sometimes associated with a grade, but not always.
- **Self-assessment:** Student assesses his or her own work and progress. Represents a form of reflection of one's own work and learning experience.

As you think about new ways to introduce multiple forms of assessment in your classroom, keep your student learning outcomes in mind. What kinds of learning do you want to occur in your class? What assessment methods will prove that learning has occurred?

P. Nightingale and other assessment experts have created eight broad categories of learning outcomes that your individual outcomes may fall under. I have matched these broad categories with some possible assessment methods that you may find useful as you brainstorm about ways to add additional assessment techniques to your classroom.[7]

Broad Outcome: Thinking critically and making judgments

This is when you want your students to be able to evaluate, assess, judge, and develop arguments. Possible assessment methods include your student
- writing a newspaper report, speech, or poem
- presenting an oral case or argument
- holding a debate or moot court session
- writing essays, reports, or a journal
- writing a letter to an editor or an advice column
- preparing a briefing for a committee or organization
- writing a book review for a particular journal or newspaper

Broad Outcome: Solving problems and developing plans

This is when you want your students to identify, pose, or define a problem, analyze data, review or design experiments, make plans, or apply information. Possible assessment methods include your student
- solving a case study
- solving a problem-based scenario
- engaging in a simulation
- engaging in a hands-on experiment
- creating a conference presentation
- creating a poster presentation

Broad Outcome: Performing procedures and demonstrating techniques

This is when you want your students to compute, use equipment, follow procedures or protocols, or carry out instructions. Possible assessment methods include your student
- demonstrating a procedure

- producing a video
- producing a podcast or vodcast
- posting a video to YouTube
- role playing
- producing a poster
- producing a presentation using multi-media
- writing a lab report
- creating a manual
- conducting a real or simulated professional practice

Broad Outcome: Managing and developing oneself

This is when you want your students to work either collaboratively or independently. You want them to be self-directed and goal-oriented and learn to manage their time, tasks, and to organize their work. Possible assessment methods include your student
- writing a journal
- keeping a diary
- creating a portfolio or an e-portfolio
- creating a learning contract

Broad Outcome: Accessing and managing information

This is when you want your students to research, investigate, interpret, and organize information. Students will collect data, search or manage information and interpret it. Possible assessment methods include your student
- writing an annotated bibliography
- creating a project
- writing a thesis or dissertation
- completing an applied task
- solving a problem

Broad Outcome: Demonstrating knowledge and understanding

This is when you want your students to recall, describe, report, recognize, identify, or relate materials. Possible assessment methods include your student
- completing a written examination
- completing an oral examination
- writing an essay
- writing a report
- writing short answer responses

- completing a multiple-choice exam
- write a minute paper
- completing a pre-test
- completing a post-test
- participating in a discussion
- writing or recording self-reflections

Broad Outcome: Designing, creating, and performing

This is when you want your students to design, create, produce, innovate, or perform. Possible assessment methods include your student
- Creating a portfolio or presentation
- Completing a project
- Participating in a performance

Broad Outcome: Communicating

This is when you want your students to engage in verbal, written, and non-verbal communicate within a group. Students will ague, advocate, interview, present, and negotiate. Possible assessment methods include your student:
- Participating in a discussion or debate
- Role playing
- Participating in a simulation
- Presenting to an audience or camera
- Writing an essay or report
- Writing a reflective paper

Most of the evaluative instruments listed above can be used as formative, summative, or self-assessments. Once you have linked an assessment method with your specific Student Learning Outcome, you will see how simple it is to move to the instructional strategy or activity. Your outcome and assessment method will point naturally to the ways in which you can teach the course content to your students.

Consider Validity

Assessment experts talk a great deal about validity. What do they mean when they ask, "is an assessment instrument valid?" Validity in assessment refers to an instrument measuring what it is supposed to measure. For example, if you want to test Music Appreciation learning outcomes that require students to relate common elements in music from different periods, your assessment instrument would not be valid if all your test questions ask the student to simply identify specific pieces of music. You would not be testing what you say you want your students to know. If your learning outcome stated that you wanted students to identify pieces of music, then your instrument would be valid. *Be sure that your assessment method measures what you intend to measure!*

To insure validity, match the assessment method (such as a test question, prompt, or portfolio) to your outcome statement and to the cognitive level that you believe best matches the intent of your learning outcome. For example, if your student learning outcome statement requires a student to recall important facts, then you must use an assessment method that tests this. For example, a multiple-choice question could accomplish this, as could a fill-in-the-blank response. But if the outcome statement requires a student to interpret or make an inference, then your assessment method must include this higher cognitive level task. For example a constructed response statement might accomplish this. Constructed responses include essays, short answers, speeches, or newspaper articles.

Whatever assessment method you choose must get at the degree to which a student has succeeded in meeting the expectations of the learning outcome.

How to Differentiate Levels or Degrees of Student Understanding

Now that you have found multiple ways in which you can measure student learning, you are ready to begin differentiating between degrees of understanding. Now you will begin to clarify the criteria for judging your students' performances. How will you determine which students "got" the material and which did not? How will you distinguish between the students who truly understood the concepts and those who simply appeared to? What criteria will you use to judge the work?

Learning for real understanding is not a right or wrong process. Learning, at least the kind we say that we want for our students, is a matter of degree. Learners are sophisticated or naïve, they are advanced or hindered, they know more or less. The type of assessment instrument you choose must also measure the degree to which a student has succeeded in meeting the expectation of the learning outcome.

Rubrics

Rubrics—or scoring guides—will assist you in evaluating the degree of quality of your students' work. Rubrics represent an effective means of judging your students along a continuum because you create them to describe a progression of skills or knowledge. Instructors that use rubrics to evaluate students' work feel confident that they are systematically evaluating their students. Additionally, instructors who give their students rubrics in advance assist their students in the learning process. Students with rubrics know exactly how they will be evaluated and can prepare accordingly. What else can rubrics do you for you?

- Improve student performance
- Make the evaluation process transparent
- Allow for objective and consistent assessment
- Help students judge their own work
- Provide students with feedback about their work

There are two kinds of rubrics that you may find particularly useful: holistic rubrics and analytic rubrics.

Holistic rubrics have only one general descriptor and provide a single score based on an instructor's impression of the student's work. For example, a test question that asks the student to *compare musical genres from two different periods* can be scored holistically by considering both the quality of information provided and the quantity against a scale. Here is an example of a holistic rubric:

Score = 1	Score = 2	Score = 3	Score = 4
Does not meet expectations	Progressing toward expectations	Meets expectations	Exceeds expectations

Use of holistic rubrics is appropriate when performance tasks require students to generate a response when there is no definitive right or wrong answer. Evaluation using a holistic rubric focuses on proficiency, quality, and understanding of specific content and associated skills. Holistic rubrics are most often associated with summative assessment and provide little feedback to the student. Advantages of holistic rubrics include:

- Are often written generically and so can be used to evaluate multiple tasks
- Save time by limiting the number of decisions a rater must make
- Have little detail so may be easily understood by unsophisticated learners

Disadvantages to holistic rubrics include:

- Do not provide specific feedback to learners about strengths and weaknesses
- Criteria cannot be differentially weighed
- Performances may meet more than one criteria, making it difficult to choose between descriptors

Analytic Rubrics have multiple rating scales, each corresponding to an independent dimension that when added together provide an overall score. While descriptors may be similar to those found in holistic rubrics, they are presented in separate categories in analytic rubrics and rated individually. These rubrics usually combine performance categories with descriptions of particular tasks to be demonstrated. Using the same example that asks the student to *compare musical genres from two different periods,* an analytic rubric could contain a rating scale from 1 to 4 and 4 elements (dimensions) for a total of up to 16 points. Here is an example of an analytic rubric:

Rating Scale					
Element (dimension)	1	2	3	4	Total
Number of comparisons	1	2	3	4	
Quality of comparisons	1	2	3	4	
Accuracy of time periods	1	2	3	4	
Correct musicians of the period	1	2	3	4	
					Total Pts:

Let's use this rubric to score a "student." After reading Bob Student's essay, we would simply indicate on each area how well he met the criteria. In this case, Bob was able to correctly identify and associate musicians with a period, but struggled to make comparisons between them.

Bob Student	Rating Scale				
Element (dimension)	1	2	3	4	Total
Number of comparisons	1	2 ✔	3	4	
Quality of comparisons	1	2 ✔	3	4	
Accuracy of time periods	1	2	3 ✔	4	
Correct musicians of the period	1	2	3	4 ✔	
					Total Pts:

The advantages of using analytic rubrics include:
• Provide useful feedback to learners on strengths and weaknesses
• Dimensions can be weighted to reflect importance

Disadvantages include:
- Take time to prepare and use
- More possibilities for raters to disagree because there are more options

General Guidelines for Writing Rubrics

Assessment and Measurement Specialist Dr. Ronald Carriveau at the University of North Texas has developed seven guidelines that will help you while writing rubrics:

1. Determine whether a holistic or analytic rubric is more appropriate for your needs. If you only want an overall score, a holistic rubric may work well for you, but if you need sub-scores to help students develop or to assist you with determining whether you need to re-teach something, an analytic rubric may work better.

2. Determine how many levels of performance you need to fit your purposes. The examples have shown four levels, but you may need only three, or perhaps more than four, depending on the situation. You will need to adjust the labels for each category and the descriptors. Be sure that the labels and levels move along a continuum.

3. Write proficiency descriptors for each level of the rubric, starting with the highest level and working down to the lowest. It is good to start with the highest level because that is the level you expect your students to achieve. Each level below the highest illustrates lower expectations. Students will have a visual cue of strengths and weaknesses depending on their placement along the continuum.

4. In your descriptor statements, focus on the presence of the quantity and quality that you expect, rather than its absence. For example, if the highest level requires four comparisons and a clear and concise response, then the next level down would require three comparisons and a moderate degree of clarity. Steer clear of negative descriptors like "comparisons are missing and description is not clear." Only the lowest level should contain elements such as "lacking" or "absent."

5. Keep the elements of the description parallel from performance level to performance level. For example, if you have included quantity, details, and clarity in one descriptor, make sure all descriptors include these same three elements.

6. Avoid the use of words that are vague such as "interesting, well done, creative, sufficient, several, numerous, great, okay."

7. Be careful to keep the descriptor somewhat generic. An overly detailed or specific descriptor may go beyond the actual learning outcome it is measuring.[8]

See the individual case study chapters (Chapters 6 to 9) for examples of rubrics developed by N-Gen Redesign faculty at the University of North Texas. These rubrics align with the course student learning outcomes, also available in the case studies.

Peer Assessments

Students given the opportunity to assess one another begin to think critically about work quality and evaluation as a process. For example, learners might be asked to determine what constitutes exemplary performance on an assignment, forcing them to engage meta-cognitively with the task and the ways in which tasks are evaluated.

Peer assessment is most productive in a supportive classroom environment where students feel comfortable and trust each other and the instructor. Otherwise, they will not provide honest or constructive feedback. Form trust in your classroom by creating small groups early during the term and keep the groups consistent throughout. Devote time to familiarizing students with the objectives for the assignments that they will be evaluating and show them how those objectives align with the learning outcomes and the key concepts in the discipline. Provide students with rubrics to guide the process. After students become familiar with using rubrics, they can begin to make their own, collaboratively, to evaluate their peers. Peer assessment can be used formatively with good results, encouraging an environment where everyone expects to learn from everyone else.

Self-Assessment

Self-assessment engages students directly with the learning process, forcing them to think deliberately about what and how they are learning. This kind of reflection creates a meta-cognitive environment that encourages higher-order thinking. It can also train students to become independent learners and can increase motivation. When you incorporate self-assessment into your course, be sure to set specific goals for students to achieve. Goals are essential so that students can evaluate their progress and can measure their progression toward mastery. While goals can be task-specific and/or over-arching, they should be realistic, short-term, and attainable.

Portfolios (either hard or electronic) can assist students with self-assessment. Portfolios are purposefully organized, systematic collections of student work that tell a story of progress, effort, and achievement. Both the instructor and the student will determine what is included in the portfolio, develop guidelines for inclusion, and criteria for judging merit. All portfolios should include a rationale for each piece included, as well as a reflective statement about progress over time.

Collaborative or Group Assessment

Group evaluation is often troubling to instructors, yet group or collaborative work mimics real-world practice more closely than possibly any other aspect of the learning environment. Teachers struggle with grading group work—should all members receive the same grade? Can individual contributions be separated from the group? What if the group doesn't get along? Additionally, students often complain about group work, yet they will engage in working in teams throughout their careers. They need practice to learn how to effectively communicate and manage group projects. One way to insure peer interaction and participation is to have group members evaluate themselves. This turns the grading of the group into another group activity. Here is an example of a peer evaluation used in a History course:

Peer Evaluation

Dimension	4	3	2	1	Total
Research and Organizes Information	Collects a great deal of information—all of which contributes to the topic.	Collects some basic information—most of which relates to the topic.	Collects or organizes little information—only some of which is relevant to the topic.	Does not collect or organize information that relates to the topic.	
Shares Information	Relays most information, all of which relates to the topic.	Relays some basic information, most of which is related to the topic.	Relays little information, only some of which is related to the topic.	Does not relay information to group.	
Values others Opinions	Listens and speaks when appropriate.	Listens, but talks too much.	Usually does most of the talking. Rarely allows others to speak.	Is always talking. Never allows other team members to speak.	
Fulfills team Role's Duties	Performs all duties of assigned team roles.	Performs nearly all the assigned duties.	Performs few of the assigned duties.	Does not perform duties of assigned team role.	
Cooperates with Teammates	Cooperates with teammates in a productive way	Cooperates most of the time with teammates	Reluctantly cooperates with teammates	Usually argues with group in a counter-productive way.	
					Total

A holistic rubric for peer assessment might allow for points to be given to students. A set number of points (or even a dollar amount, for example) limits students and forces them to think more closely about peer participation. An example of a holistic rubric is shown below:

Holistic Peer Evaluation

Criteria	Name	Name	Name	Name	Total
Organized					
Level of participation					
Met deadlines					
Worked with the group					
Showed up for meetings					
					Total

Aligning Assessments with Outcomes

Now that you have your student learning outcomes and your assessments determined, it is time to ensure that they align. Remember that the goal of assessment is to ensure that all students are meeting the course objectives (identified by the student learning outcomes).

Alignment is easiest to ensure when the student learning outcomes are plotted onto a matrix or blueprint. This blueprint becomes the basis of the assessment plan, ensuring that assessments align with outcomes and also that the SLOs and assessments address varying degrees of cognitive difficulty. Areas to think about while you are plotting the blueprint:
• Are there outcomes not associated with an assessment?
• Are there assessments that do not contribute to an outcome?
• Are appropriate cognitive levels addressed for each outcome?
• Have we included practice on the outcome prior to requiring mastery?
• If "yes" is a response to any of the above, do you change the outcome, the assessment, or the teaching strategy?

Below is a sample assessment blueprint. On this sample, you insert your goal and student learning outcomes in the left two columns. Record each assessment item under the cognitive levels, depending on whether they are low, medium, or high, and then calculate the number of assessment items you have per learning outcome. Be sure to record what assessment item "type" you are using so that you are certain that you have a variety of assessment measures that are self-, formative, and summative. For example, your "types" might include multiple-choice or constructed response items.

Assessment Blueprint

		Cognitive Levels			
	Item Difficulty	Low	Medium	High	
	Cognitive category	Literal/Factual/Recall	Interpretive/Inferential	Critical-thinking/Evaluative	Items per Outcome Type
Learning Outcomes					
Goal 1					
	Outcome 1				
	Outcome2				
	Outcome3				
Goal 2					
	Outcome 1				
	Outcome 2				
	Outcome 3				
Goal 3					
	Outcome 1				
	Outcome 2				
Goal 4					
	Outcome 1				
	Outcome 2				
	Outcome 3				
	Outcome 4				
					Total

An Assessment System Model

Your assessment blueprint now forms the basis of your assessment plan, which is a key component in your assessment system. An assessment system is comprised of these things:
- Student learning outcomes
- Assessment and evaluation
- Instructional activities
- Validity evidence

An assessment system is simply a collection of assessment tools that measure performance, define who will evaluate that performance, and describe the performance to be evaluated. The system also indicates how often the evaluation will occur. All systems should use multiple forms of evaluation and be delivered fairly. Your assessment system will enable you to decide how you should best approach "teaching" your content to your students. In essence, the data gathered from your assessment system will enable you to make good instructional decisions.[9]

An Assessment System Model

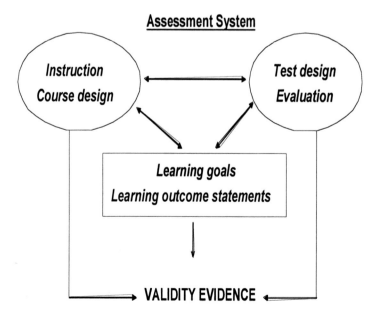

Assessment System

Instruction
Course design

Test design
Evaluation

Learning goals
Learning outcome statements

VALIDITY EVIDENCE

You now have the first two components of your assessment system: student learning outcomes and assessments. You are now ready to start matching your outcomes and assessments with instructional strategies. How will you teach your students the course content?

After reading this Chapter, you should have . . .
1. determined specifically which assessments you will use in your course. Be sure to include both formative and summative assessments.
2. created specific assessment items (multiple choice questions, essay questions, project assignments, paper assignments, etc.).
3. aligned the specific assessment item to the Student Learning Outcome.
4. used this alignment to create an Assessment Blue Print for the course.

C H A P T E R   F I V E

Learning Strategies, Course Structure, and How People Learn

What We Know about How People Learn

What is learning? How do we engage in learning? Systematic research into the human mind using scientific methods began in the late nineteenth century with behaviorists who believed that learning was a process of connections formed between stimuli and responses. More recent studies have defined learning as the "stabilizing, through repeated use, of certain appropriate and desirable synapses in the brain." Others have argued that learning is "a way of interacting with the world. As we learn, our conceptions of phenomena change, and we see the world differently."[1]

Although learning has been defined in a variety of ways and remains an elusive act that proves difficult to measure, research has shown that WHAT students learn is largely determined by HOW they learn. Paul Ramsden, a professor at the Institute of Higher Education at Griffith University in Brisbane, Australia, says that:

> *What* students learn is indeed closely associated with *how* they go about learning it. It does not seem to matter whether the approaches are measured by means of questionnaires or interviews, whether the subject area is engineering or history or medicine, or whether the outcomes are defined in terms of grades or in terms of some qualitative measure of learning. . . .[2]

The approach, Ramsden argues, "is not about learning facts versus learning concepts: It is about learning *just* the unrelated facts (or procedures) versus learning the facts *in relation to* the concepts. Surface [learning] is, at best, about quantity without quality; deep [learning] is about quality and quantity."[3]

None of us engage in surface learning in the "real" world. Surface approaches to learning are artificial and are the result of particular kinds of learning environments that reward that approach. For example, students who do well memorizing facts and repeating them on tests are rewarded with good grades. Good grades are one of the primary pieces of evidence of "success" in school. Students soon realize that if they want to succeed—they must only memorize and repeat. School quickly becomes an artificial environment for surface learning.

Ramsden has elaborated at length about how school environments can foster surface learning:

> Surface approaches have nothing to do with wisdom and everything to do with aimless accumulation. They belong to an artificial world of learning, where faithfully reproducing fragments of torpid knowledge to please teachers and pass examinations has replaced understanding. Paralysis of thought leads inevitably to misunderstandings of important principles, weak long-term recall of detail, and inability to apply academic knowledge to the real world. A surface approach shows itself in different ways in different subject areas, but lead down the same desolate road in every field, from mathematics to fine arts. Once the material learned in this way is reproduced as required, it is soon forgotten, and it never becomes part of the students' way of interpreting the universe.[4]

We can change the kinds of learning students engage in—surface versus deep—by changing the learning environment. Learning environments are made up in part of teaching strategies. This chapter will help to make you more aware of the types of teaching strategies that exist, particularly the strategies that can promote a deeper orientation to learning.

In my experience—informed by both practice and the literature on learning—the teaching strategies that promote the kind of deep learning that we want our students to engage in are active in nature. Active learning results from teaching strategies that encourage students to talk, listen, read, write, and reflect through specific activities such as solving problems, working on case studies, and role-playing.

Active Learning

Most learning that occurs in colleges today is of a passive nature. Students sit through a lecture listening and, perhaps, taking notes. Little to no interaction occurs between the student and the instructor or between the students. Students may *think* about the content, but they do not *do* anything with the content. In a passive learning environment, students are never actively engaged with the content in a meaningful way. As Arthur Chickering and Zelda Gamson contend in *Applying the Seven Principles for Good Practice in Undergraduate Education*, "Learning is not a spectator sport. Students do not learn much just by sitting in classes listening to teachers, memorizing pre-packaged assignments, and spitting out answers." They must talk about what they are learning, write about it, relate it to past experiences, apply it to their daily lives. They must make what they learn part of themselves." Christopher J. Lucas and John W. Murray have pointed out in their book, *New Faculty: A Practical Guide for Academic Beginners*, "learning should be thought of as a verb rather than as a noun. Learning, properly considered, is an action process, with students doing and thinking."[5]

What is active learning? Active learning is any kind of learning that involves students *doing* things rather than *thinking* about doing things.

Experiential Learning

Experiential Learning is learning through direct experience. Students engage in hands-on encounters with the phenomena being studied, rather than merely thinking about the phenomena, or they participate directly in life-events.[6]

David Kolb, professor of Organizational Behavior in the Weatheread School of Management, is one of the pioneering proponents of experiential learning. Kolb, along with colleague Roger Fry, created a model that represents the four elements of experiential learning experiences. The model below shows the inter-relationships of the learning process. Kolb and Fry argue that learning can begin at any point and should be considered a continuous circle.

Active, experientially-based learning forms a large umbrella under which lie multiple kinds of learning strategies.[7] While more active learning strategies exist than these, the following will be reviewed in this book:
- Problem-based learning
- Case-based learning
- Discussion and debate
- Role-playing
- Clickers

Tips for using active learning in your classroom:
- Be creative about the kinds of active learning you use.
- Provide students with the resources they need or the means to get the resources.
- Allow plenty of time to complete the activity.
- Do not step in and direct the students.
- Observe student interactions and provide feedback after the activity is completed.
- Give students specific roles if you are concerned about participation.
- Rotate student roles if multiple activities are planned for the course.
- Encourage students to communicate outside of class.
- Be available to answer student questions.
- Make a clear connection between the activity and the course learning outcomes.
- Give students the scoring rubrics in advance of the activity.

Problem-Based Learning

Problem-based learning, known as PBL, most often involves the assignment of a specific problem that must be solved by students, typically in groups. Students research the topic, assess the situation, consider various options, and offer a final solution to the problem.

PBL emerged in medical schools to encourage students to apply the knowledge that they were learning in the classroom. Some universities have invested considerable resources into the development of PBL courses. The University of Delaware is perhaps the most prominent, in part because it hosts a PBL Clearinghouse that supplies examples of classroom activities for different subject areas, along with articles by faculty who have taught PBL courses. As policy makers and corporations increase demands for accountability in higher education, especially in the realm of preparing college students for future careers, PBL will continue to grow as a means of providing students with active, engaging, "real world" training. At the same time, PBL is also effective in helping students learn course content and improve their ability to participate actively in the learning process. Most subject areas are conducive to this type of approach, but few disciplines actually take advantage of the PBL method.

Why should you use problem-based learning as a primary teaching strategy?
- To emphasize a major concept that is central to the course
- To give students practice with leading discussions
- To highlight a flawed or imperfect situation that relates to the course
- To help students think creatively and strategically
- To prepare students for life outside of the classroom

There are several ways in which you can incorporate problem-based learning in your classroom. These include:
- Assign a small group project that must be completed within a single class meeting. Large classes can be sub-divided into small groups to accomplish this.
- Create a large group project that spans multiple class periods. Students will engage in the project both in and outside of class.
- Develop your entire course around problem-based learning
- Find specific examples of problem-based activities at the University of Delaware's PBL Clearinghouse (https://chico.nss.udel.edu/Pbl/).

Some of the challenges of using problem-based learning include:
- Overly complicated or overly simplistic problems
- Not differentiating between general problem-solving and problem-based learning
- Students who dominate discussions or do not participate
- The tendency to insert a PBL activity into an existing course structure without modifying the rest of the course to accommodate the time needed for the activity

Some solutions to the challenges include:
- Make sure that there is an actual problem that must be solved.
- Assign specific roles to students to ensure proper participation and group dynamics.
- Cut or condense lecture material to accommodate PBL activities.
- Provide clear guidelines to students.

Case Study Learning

Case study learning involves using a specific example to illustrate a theoretical concept. Scholarly authors often use case studies to share their own experiences, but case studies can also be used to enhance student learning. All case studies include a detailed narrative description of a situation that involves fictitious or real people. Engaging in the case study allows students to consider "real world" issues they might encounter outside the classroom. Although case studies may be seen as a subset of problem-based learning, not all cases require students to propose a solution. In fact, sometimes the solution has already been carried out.

Like problem-based learning, the case study approach is closely tied to medical and science education. In fields where students will eventually be expected to make decisions based on examination and methodical research, case studies offer students the chance to practice and develop these skills. Law is another field where case studies have thrived because students can analyze actual court cases for merits and flaws in the ruling. Outside of these areas (except business), case studies are less prominent but should be used more widely because cases provide opportunities for practical application of content.[8]

Writing case studies can be challenging. Clyde Freedman Herreid, an expert in the case study method, recommends these tips for building an effective case:[9]
1. Provide a clear narrative plot with a beginning, middle, and end.
2. Choose a captivating topic to engage students.
3. Choose a recent topic for current relevance (especially when dealing with the sciences).
4. Generate empathy with the central characters.
5. Provide quotations from primary sources for realism.
6. Provide a clear narrative plot with a beginning, middle, and end.
7. Choose a captivating topic to engage students.
8. Choose a recent topic for current relevance (especially when dealing with the sciences).
9. Generate empathy with the central characters.
10. Provide quotations from primary sources for realism.
11. Find cases that are similar to situations that students might encounter.
12. Ensure that the case serves a pedagogical function.
13. Choose a case that includes some sort of controversy to generate discussion.
14. Find issues that require students to make a decision.
15. Use cases that can be applied to broader issues beyond the specific narrative.
16. Provide short cases to hold student attention.

What should a good case study include?
1. Elements of a case:
    a. <u>Characters</u>: Describe the characters involved in the situation. Explain their background, education, current roles and responsibilities, challenges, ideologies, positions in a larger workforce and/or social structure, ethical dilemmas, and other useful information. Make the characters come alive.
    b. <u>Situation</u>: Identify the current circumstance that students must examine. List any companies, agencies, civic organizations, social groups, and objects/products that figure into the case. Also explain any laws, regulations, and policies that are relevant. If students must solve a problem—define the problem.

c. <u>Outcome(s)</u>: If the case is "closed" (an action has resolved the case, either positively or negatively), explain the outcome so that students may analyze major decisions that the characters made. If the case is "open-ended," ask students to posit different resolutions, including benefits and consequences. Ask students what they would do in that circumstance and then have them identify instances in the narrative where a different decision could have affected the outcome.

What kinds of situations make for good cases?
- Policy decisions that must be made or that have already been implemented.
- A description of a catastrophe where students examine the decisions and actions leading up to the crisis.
- A classroom educational situation or school board meeting.
- A business or marketing plan.
- An examination of a computer virus and what allowed it to spread.
- A historical event that has received a new interpretation.

Why should you use case study learning as a primary teaching strategy?
- Provides student with the opportunity to analyze actions and decision in real-life or hypothetical situations.
- Encourages student empathy with the individuals involved in the case.
- Helps students understand the complexities of real-life situations.

There are several ways in which you can incorporate case study learning in your classroom. These include:
- During a lecture, introduce a "closed" case (one already resolved) and allow the class the discuss it.
- Assign a short case with all supporting materials intact. Students complete the case in a single class period.
- Assign a lengthy, open-ended case that requires students to gather information. Much of the work will be completed outside of class.
- Allow students to develop their own case studies.

Some of the challenges of using case study learning include:
- Giving students cases without enough contextual details or with too many irrelevant details.
- Giving students cases that are outdated or irrelevant.
- Giving students cases that are not clearly connected with the learning outcomes.
- Student uncertainty about how they will be assessed during the learning.

Some solutions to the challenges include:
- Think of case study writing as story-telling. What kinds of questions might the case generate?
- Keep cases current by updating them periodically.
- Provide students with a rubric, a clear set of expectations, and immediate feedback.
- Create individual writing assignments for the case studies so that students are individually responsible, particularly if these assignments are reflective in nature.

Discussion and Debate

Discussion and debate are learning strategies where students are led through a series of questions and topics logically to allow for the understanding of complex topics. Students will think about the issues on their own and form their own insights and judgments.

Classroom Discussion

Instructors who use discussion in class are engaging to some degree in the "Socratic Method" of teaching—where an instructor asks students a series of questions in a logical order to lead to understanding. In its purest form, instructors would only pose questions and never provide answers or information to students. Pure Socratic methods are rarely used in class and most instructors take the thrust of the method—teaching through questioning—and mold "discussions."

In a classroom discussion, the instructor may or may not "lead" the class through a discussion and even if the instructor does so at the beginning, he or she should be ready to move aside as soon as possible, leaving the role of expert and becoming a facilitator. Why should you use discussion as a primary teaching strategy?
- Students will become engaged with a diverse number of ideas in a meaningful way.
- Students will have the opportunity to "teach" others.
- Actively questioning the material opens new avenues of exploration.

There are several ways in which you can incorporate discussion in your classroom. These include:
- Alternating lecture with short discussions.
- Beginning new assignments with discussion questions.
- Asking students to respond in writing to a question at the end of class period and then beginning the next class with that question and students' responses.

Some of the challenges of using case study learning include:
- Extremely vocal students may dominate a discussion.
- Large classes might make it difficult for all students to respond to questions.
- Class clowns might try to lead the discussion off-topic.
- No one responds to questions.

Some solutions to the challenges include:
- Talk with vocal students and enlist their assistance in allowing everyone to participate.
- Break large classes into small groups and have small groups discuss and then report out to the larger class.
- Elect discussion leaders for groups who are responsible for jump-starting small-group discussions.
- Establish a discussion protocol at the beginning of the course, with which all students agree, that with that will maintain the intellectual focus of discussions.
- Wait at least 30 seconds after posing a question for students to respond. Become comfortable with silence. Many students are trying to formulate a response and just need SILENCE before responding.
- Pose discussion questions in advance so that students can prepare ahead of time.

Debate

Debate is a type of discussion activity that engages students by requiring them to argue for or against a set position. Debates work best when students are presented with a topic that is controversial or that challenges their existing beliefs and opinions. If students are assigned to work with a group during the debate, student leaders can represent the others by speaking for the group. Opening arguments will present the main points, and each group will offer rebuttals in response. During the conclusion, each group will restate the main points as well as the reasons for opposition to the other groups' points.

In *Discussion as a Way of Teaching: Tools and Techniques for Democratic Classrooms*, Stephen D. Brookfield and Stephen Preskill offer a method of conducting a "critical debate" in the classroom.[10] The basic steps involve:
1. Identify a contentious issue on which students have divided opinions.
2. Propose the issue and ask for students to volunteer for sides.
3. Assign students to the opposite side than that for which they originally volunteered.
4. Conduct the debate with peer selected group leaders for opening arguments and rebuttals.

5. Debrief the debate and ask students to comment on the challenges of arguing an unfamiliar side.
6. Assign a follow-up reflection paper where students can address the issues raised by the debate and how their perspectives changed.

Why should you use debate as a primary teaching strategy?
• Challenges students' pre-conceived notions about a topic.
• Allows students to consider other perspectives on topics and to think creatively.
• Helps students gain empathy for others.
• Reinforces concepts and relationships between concepts.

There are several ways in which you can incorporate debate in your classroom. These include:
• Divide the classroom and provide a debate topic. Students research the topic and come to class prepared to argue both positions. Their assigned positions are announced at the beginning of the class.
• At the end of a unit of study, divide the classroom and provide the debate topic and positions. Have students debate using only the materials they have with them and from the knowledge they have gained during the study of the unit. This form of debate can serve as a review. Allow the students time during the class to prepare as a group before making arguments (perhaps 20 minutes of preparation for a 40 minute debate).
• Use online discussion boards and time outside of class to prepare for a debate that will happen in-class, online on a discussion board, or Wiki.

Some of the challenges of using debate include:
• One side of the argument may appear to students to be easier to argue than the other.
• Students may be extremely opposed to one of the argument.
• Personal experiences may cause students to lose their intellectual distance from a topic.
• Students may argue "around" the topic rather than addressing it directly.
• Antagonistic students may create a hostile and untrustworthy environment.

Some solutions to the challenges include:
• Establish good rapport between instructor/students and students/students during the course to create a safe environment for intellectual pursuits.

- "Debrief" after the debate to discuss the topics, points-of-view, and how students' personal opinions may have differed from their assigned positions, and to clarify misconceptions and "wrong" information.
- Establish a protocol with students for courteous behavior during debates.
- The instructor should not interfere or interject his/her opinions into the student debate.

Role-Playing

Role-playing can be used for teaching when students assume a specific role to simulate a scenario. In the classroom, students can work through a situation and practice behavior for the real world. Alternatively, the role-playing activities may be used to shed light on any complicated topic. To be effective, students must take on the roles that they are assigned and assume the vantage point of a specific character. Some students may play themselves while others are given roles that require them to behave in ways in which they would not normally.

Role-playing allows for creativity in the classroom. Used for many years by political strategists and in business training, role-playing is now incorporated by many disciplines because it allows students to act out a given scenario in "real time" and encourages collaborative work between students.

Morry Van Ments in *The Effective Use of Role-play: Practical Techniques for Improving Learning*, outlines a strategy for planning and executing a role-play activity. This book offers guidelines for incorporating role-play in the classroom, including detailed advice for different classroom situations.[11] The basic steps involve:
1. Setting objectives for role-play activity.
2. Establishing what constraints are posed on the students or the situation.
3. Identifying critical factors for students to address and understand.
4. Deciding how to structure the activity preparation and "play."
5. Selecting materials for students to read to prepare and to provide context.
6. Running the role-playing activity in-class or online.
7. De-briefing students after the activity.
8. Following-up with subsequent activities and assessments to determine learning.

Why should you use role-playing as a primary teaching strategy?
- Allows students to experience or practice a situation that they might eventually encounter in their lives.
- Helps students to empathize with others.
- Can change attitudes and behaviors.

- Enables students to experience different perspectives and think creatively.
- Allows students to engage content directly in a meaningful way.

There are several ways in which you can incorporate role-playing in your classroom. These include:
- Have students engage in a demonstration or teaching activity with assigned roles.
- Modify a case study to have students "play" assigned roles from the case.
- Have students create roles and a scenario to "play" based on lecture materials.

Some of the challenges of using role-playing include:
- Factual information may seem to be downplayed.
- Emotional responses can create conflict or take students off-topic.
- Requires preparation and commitment on the students' part.
- Can be time-consuming.
- Students may not recognize that learning is taking place.

Some solutions to the challenges include:
- Hold a "debriefing" after the role-play to demonstrate the direct link between the role-play and the learning outcomes and to correct any misconceptions.
- Allow sufficient time during the course for preparation and play. Do not try and "attach" a role-play onto the existing class. Make role-play a primary teaching activity.
- Cut lecture time and allow the role-playing to introduce concepts and materials.
- Provide clear rubrics for learning expectations and for student behavior.
- Take into account that some roles will require more from students than others will.
- Be prepared for student questions or resistance. Explain to them why the activity is important.
- Choose topics that will help students become better critical thinkers or that will allow them to gain empathy.

Clickers

Clickers, or student response systems (SRSs), have been around in various guises since the 1960s. Clickers allow instructors to assess students through a handheld keypad that typically looks like a remote control device. A receiver at the front of the classroom allows software on a computer to record the results. Instructors may also display the results so that students can compare answers with their peers and track classroom learning. Some instructors also use clickers to record attendance.

Research has shown that clickers can be used with great effect in large lecture classes to encourage student participation and to formatively assess student understanding. The use of clickers should be determined based on course objectives that align with the student learning outcomes.[12]

Researchers measuring the effectiveness of clickers in science classes have developed general recommendations for their use in the classroom:[13]
1. Use the clickers in ways that are unique compared to traditional paper tasks.
2. Become comfortable with the technology before using the clickers in front of a class.
3. Choose a product that is simple to use and does not demand a lot of your time to master.
4. Allow students to assume new empowering roles in the classroom through use of clickers.
5. Clarify the guidelines for student work through instructions, rubrics, and formats for group work.

Why should you use clickers as a primary teaching strategy?
*   Can invigorate a lecture by breaking it up into small chunks.
*   Introduces an element of active learning to lectures.
*   Allows an instructor to assess understanding of materials during a lecture. Instructors can then recover materials not grasped in a different format.
*   Allows for collaborative learning during lectures when students are paired and asked to discuss questions before responding with clickers.
*   Allows students to project occurrences or questions prior to lecture. Pretests knowledge or misconceptions.

There are several ways in which you can incorporate clickers in your classroom. These include:
*   Build lectures around key questions. Stop the lecture, ask question, allow students to discuss in pairs or small groups, then have them respond via clicker.
*   Use student responses to illustrate misconceptions or misunderstandings. Can demonstrate how great a misunderstanding might be over a concept.
*   Begin a lecture with a posed question and have students respond. This will introduce the topic in a dynamic way.
*   Use as a "gaming" tool in a small class—much like Jeopardy.

Some of the challenges of using clickers include:
*   Maintenance issues—do you distribute clickers each class? What if students lose their clicker?

- Costs of clickers and other associated equipment.
- Training time for instructors in how to use the technology.
- Effectively introducing questions and activities into the lecture for use with clickers.

Some solutions to the challenges include:
- Develop a firm maintenance policy for clickers prior to the class.
- Become comfortable with the technology before introducing it to students.
- Have a back-up plan in case the technology does not work.
- Create mini-lectures around key questions you will pose.
- In addition to individual student questions, use clickers to generate small group discussion and debate about conceptual issues.
- During exam reviews, use clickers for in-class games, such as Jeopardy or Trivial Pursuit, perhaps dividing the class into teams.

Additional tips for using clickers effectively in class:
- At the beginning of the semester, spend time training students to use the technology.
- Determine the consequence for students who do not bring the clicker to class.
- Rehearse your lecture in advance for timing.
- Make the clickers a regular part of the course, rather than using them occasionally.
- Allow students adequate time to answer questions.
- Set aside time for reviewing and discussing the answers.
- Tie questions to the lecture, outside reading, and student learning outcomes.
- Ask important questions to assess student learning.
- Limit the number of questions that you ask during a given lecture, generally to no more than five.
- Vary your questions.
- Space the questions throughout the lecture.
- Use a consistent format for quiz questions.
- Be creative!

Group Work

We know that students learn best when they are actively involved in the process. We also know that students tend to learn more of what is taught and retain what they learn longer when they work in small groups as compared with when the same content is delivered via lecture. Additionally, students who learn collaboratively (in groups) are more satisfied with their coursework than those who learn alone.[14]

A variety of names define this form of teaching and there are distinctions between each of the types:

- Cooperative learning
- Collaborative learning
- Collective learning
- Learning communities
- Peer teaching
- Peer learning
- Reciprocal learning
- Team learning
- Study circles
- Study groups
- Work groups

Generally, the varying types can be broken into three main categories:
- Informal learning groups: temporary, ad hoc clusters of students gathered during a single class session.
- Formal learning groups: teams created for a long-term assignment or for the entire course period.
- Study teams: long-term groups with stable-memberships that provide support, encouragement, and assistance in completing course assignments.

Small group work can assist with a variety of critical educational outcomes, but must be planned accordingly to be implemented successfully in class. Expect some student resistance to group work because some students may have been part of ill-structured groups in other classes that did not function correctly. You must assure students that everyone will participate or be penalized. Convey to students that the group activities will be well-planned. Michaelsen, Fink, and Knight list several factors that can adversely affect group work:[15]
- Shyness
- Individuals who dominate the discussion
- Lack of preparation and/or content knowledge
- Lack of commitment to group success
- Inappropriate tasks
- Students not prepared to participate actively
- Instructors sense of losing control of the class
- Time constraints

Why should you use group-work as a primary teaching strategy?
- Allows more students to actively participate in an assignment or discussion.
- Has the potential to engage in active learning for better retention of course materials.
- Develops interpersonal and team skills.

- Provides opportunities for social interaction and building team skills.
- Mimics the work environment where teams are the norm.

How can you implement group work in your course?
- Plan carefully ahead of time: include student preparation time, sequenced activities, and careful assessments that promote both individual and group accountability.
- Create tasks for groups that require interdependence.
- Include a rationale for your use of group work in your syllabus that also explains group procedures and expectations.
- Make the tasks that engage groups relevant.
- Create tasks that match student abilities and interests.
- Assign group tasks for a fair distribution of the labor.
- Create "competitions" between groups

There are several ways to create groups. Groups that are used for small assignments can be formed simply by having the students turn to a neighbor. For long-term learning groups, faculty should consider the attributes of the students when assigning them to a group. Criteria such as academic preparation and achievement, gender, and ethnicity should be heterogeneous in each group. These long term groups should be together for at least half the semester so they will have time to get to know and trust each other.

In formal groups, every student should play a specific role and roles should be rotated frequently to fairly distribute work and to provide each student with practice in the various communication and leadership tasks. Some roles to be included in groups are: facilitator, recorder, leader, reporter, and timekeeper.

One low risk strategy to implementing group work in any size classroom is "Think, Pair, Share."[16] In "Think, Pair, Share," a question is posed and written down by each person, along with their thoughts on the matter. The question should not be simple recall but should require synthesis of the course material to respond. Once everyone has written a response, they turn to someone near them and share their responses.

Think, Pair, Share can be extended and modified to fit many situations. For example, for a longer assignment, the "think" part of the strategy can be homework that has to be done before a student is allowed to participate in a group share activity. To increase individual accountability, each person's initial thoughts can be turned in for a grade.

Michaelson and Black suggest these characteristics for effective group assignments:[17]
- Require a tangible product for assessment.

- The task should be impossible to complete unless the course concepts are understood.
- Be difficult enough that a few students cannot complete the assignment working alone.
- Maximize activities that are best done in groups, such as identifying problems, formulating strategies, processing information, and making decisions. Should minimize activities that are best done alone, such as writing.
- Provide practice for future courses or jobs.
- Be interesting and/or fun.

Team Learning

Team Learning is a subset of group work. According to L. Dee Fink, "'team-based learning' is a particular instructional strategy that is designed to (a) support the development of high-performance learning teams, and (b) provide opportunities for these teams to engage in significant learning tasks." He stresses that team activities must constitute the overarching teaching strategy throughout the entire course, rather than just being used occasionally. Teams are constructed for long-term interaction so that individual members feel committed to the team and the challenging tasks that they will be required to complete. Team-based learning in this format was designed by Fink and others at the University of Oklahoma specifically to address the challenges inherent in large classes.[18]

Team-based learning tends to be applied more frequently in the sciences and the medical profession, but proponents argue that this approach can be used by a variety of disciplines. According to Fink, the greatest inhibitors to team-based learning include:[19]
- Faculty uncertainty about whether the learning objectives of a course will move beyond memorization.
- Faculty who feel threatened by challenges from students.
- Faculty who would feel that teaching is unrewarding without the "performance" nature of lecturing.
- A lack of time to commit to transforming a course to one that is team-based.

Why should you use team-based learning as a primary teaching strategy?
- Offers students training experiences that are similar to the real world.
- Provides opportunities for application of course concepts.
- Allows students to practice working with complex intellectual tasks.
- Offers students opportunities to teach or learn from their peers.

How can you implement team-based learning in your course?
- Assign teams at the beginning of the semester and have teams meet regularly during class to work on activities.
- Combine team-based learning with problem-based learning to engage in debate, role-play, or case studies.

Some of the challenges of using team-based learning include:
- Students might divide work instead of working as a team.
- Students may be concerned that some team members will not pull their weight in the group.
- Grading can be difficult.
- Some students may feel that they are not being "taught" by the instructor.
- Students may not come to class prepared to be effective team members.

Some solutions to the challenges include:
- Create assignments that make completion impossible unless students have worked together.
- Use peer evaluations so that team members can express concerns about other members.
- Create teams that last the entire semester (usually with 5 to 7 members) to build cohesion and trust.
- Build individual assignments into the group work so that students will be graded both individually and as part of a team.
- Administer pre-tests to determine whether students are prepared to work on a task.
- Instructor should assign teams rather than letting students self-select.
- Allow a team to appeal a grade, as long as they can justify their appeal.
- Support assignments with outside readings and feedback throughout the task.

Tips for using team-based learning effectively:
1. The entire course should be designed to implement team-based learning.
2. Student learning outcomes must be tied to the team activities.
3. All students in the course must work on the exact same task.
4. Team-based activities should be confined to classroom meeting times (and possibly online correspondence), rather than requiring meetings outside of class.
5. Instructor feedback must be ongoing (formative) and immediate upon completing an assignment.
6. Consider requiring students to keep journals to reflect on their role in the team and the team's activities.

In "Getting Started with Team-Based Learning," Larry K. Michaelsen lists four essential principles for team-based learning:

1. Groups must be properly formed and managed.
2. Students must be made accountable for their individual and group work.
3. Group assignments must promote both learning and team development.
4. Students must have frequent and timely performance feedback.[20]

In order to engage all students in the learning process, Larry K. Michaelsen and Arletta Bauman Knight recommend the use of the "3 S's":

1. <u>Same problem</u>: Individuals/groups should work on the same problem, case, or question.
2. <u>Specific choice</u>: Individuals/groups should be required to use course concepts to make a specific choice.
3. <u>Simultaneously report</u>: If possible, individuals/groups should report their choices simultaneously.[21]

How you Will Teach the Material

Now that you have some sense of the different kinds of active learning strategies available and how they might be used in concert with groups or teams to create a collaborative, deep-learning oriented classroom environment, it's time to make decisions about the teaching strategies you will implement in the classroom.

Academic Achievement Model

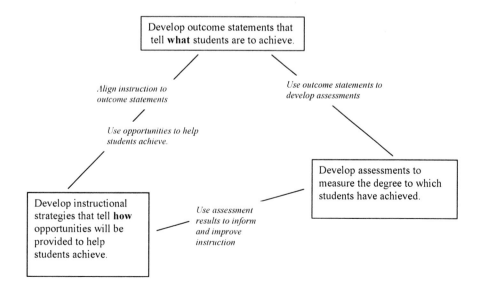

Pull out the student learning outcomes that you wrote while reading Chapter Three and the Assessment Blueprint you created during Chapter Four. What teaching strategies best fit with your learning outcomes and the items that you want to assess? Use the following worksheet to help you plan instructional activities to "teach" your learning outcomes. Be sure that your instructional activities align with your outcomes and can be assessed by using the types of assessment methods you have detailed on your Assessment Blueprint. Do you need to modify your assessment plan? Modify your learning outcome?

These are all "living" documents that you will be modifying, adapting, and changing as you plan and teach the course material. None of these documents are set in stone and can (and should!) be changed so that student learning is optimized. The only "rule" is to insure that the three components are aligned. Did students learn what you intended them to learn? Check for alignment as you fill in the Instructional Activities Checklist. If you find that one of your components is not aligned, go back and change that item. For example, you might need to modify your learning outcome because you have realized that it doesn't describe exactly what you wanted your students to learn. Once you have your instructional activities determined and aligned with your learning outcomes and assessments, you are ready to pilot your assessment system with your students.

Instructional Activities Checklist

Learning Outcome:	Assessment (how I will assess this outcome):	Teaching Strategy:	Checklist:
			How will the student learn the information and ideas in the content?
			How will the student interact actively with the content?
How does this outcome fit into the overall course content?		Justification for using this Strategy:	How will the student observe others interacting with and modeling the content?
			How will the student reflect on the content and his/her engagement with it?
			How will the student dialogue with others about the content?

Other Things to Consider

You have the basics covered and now have time to consider other elements that encourage deep-learning classroom environments.

Student Learning Styles

You are likely familiar with student learning styles, or the idea that a student may prefer one learning method more than another. Dispositions toward learning have been defined by A. F. Grasha in *Teaching with Style* as "personal qualities that influence a student's ability to acquire information, to interact with peers and the teacher, and otherwise participate in learning experiences."[22] Being aware of differing learning styles can aid the learning process as can being aware of your own learning style because there appears to be a direct correlation between a teacher's learning style and his or her own teaching style. Remember that just because you learn well using a particular method does not mean that others will, too.

What are some of the documented learning styles? Learning preferences include:
- Auditory Learners: These students prefer oral instructions. They learn by listening and speaking and enjoy talking in class.
- Visual Learners: These students prefer written instructions and easily recall what they see. They learn by observing.
- Tactile Learners: These students understand directions best when they write them. They learn best by using manipulatives and through touch.
- Kinesthetic Learners: These students also learn by touch and like to involve their whole body in learning. They learn best by acting out.
- Global Learners: These students require information to be presented in an interesting way using attractive materials. They are spontaneous and intuitive and do not like to be bored. They prefer cooperative learning activities.
- Analytic Learners: These students focus on detail and are highly logical. They plan and organize their work and prefer to work alone.
- Active Learners: These students learn best by doing something with the content they are learning.
- Reflective Learners: These students need to think about the content by themselves before they are prepared to actively do something with it.

Take the *Index of Learning Styles Questionnaire* developed by Richard M. Felder and Barbara A. Soloman at North Carolina State University online at http://www.engr.ncsu.edu/learningstyles/ilsweb.html to discover your own learning preferences. Remember to include teaching activities and assessments that appeal to a variety of student learning styles.[23]

Teaching Critical Thinking

Most instructors want to teach their students to gather, evaluate, and use information effectively. In other words, they want their students to become critical thinkers, but teaching critical thinking is a lot harder than talking about teaching critical thinking. Breaking down the skills involved in critical thinking makes the process more manageable.[24]

Skills involved in thinking critically include:
- Finding analogies or relationships between pieces of information.
- Finding and evaluating alternative solutions to problems.
- Determining the importance or validity of information that can be used to structure and solve problems.

Teaching strategies that develop these skills include:
- Open-ended questions. Asking questions that do not assume a single "right" answer. Create problems for students to work on that are ill-defined and open-ended. Students should be allowed to think and to respond creatively to the problem without fear of getting it "wrong."
- Allow time for reflection. Students need time to think about the problem—to deliberate and ponder and try out a variety of solutions before needing to respond.
- Teach for transfer. Show students how their newly acquired knowledge and skills relate to other situations and how they can apply this information to their lives.
- Group and collaborative work. Interaction among students helps each individual learn more.

Course Structures That Will Work for You: Face-to-Face, Online, Blended

It is often difficult to give your students the time they need to work on problems collaboratively if you are following the typical college course structure. If you have some flexibility in how you structure your course, you may want to consider eliminating some of your face-to-face meetings, replacing them with an online component to create a blended (or hybrid) course. Doing so can free valuable time for your students to meet, work on projects, or be actively engaged with your course content.

Blended course structures are particularly effective when used with large enrollment classes because they allow the instructor to break down a large class into small groups and then rotate the small groups through the classroom.

For example, a class of 100 students could be broken into 4 small groups of 25 students (groups A, B, C, and D) that meet every Monday, Wednesday, and Friday. The instructor has divided the content into 8 units and each unit lasts 2 weeks. Every student attends class on Mondays and participates in a clicker-enabled lecture given by the professor. The student has a problem-based assignment to work on during the rest of the unit and attends class on their "designated group day" to participate in the active in-class portion of the assignment. The schedule would look like this:

Class Schedule for Unit (Units last two weeks)	Monday	Wednesday	Friday
Unit 1	Lecture: All Attend	Group A	Group B
	Lecture: All Attend	Group C	Group D
Unit 2	Lecture: All Attend	Group A	Group B
	Lecture: All Attend	Group C	Group D

Part of climbing "out of the box" with course redesign includes thinking carefully about how often you need to meet face-to-face with your students and what kind of course structure might work best for optimal student learning. It may be that your students need to spend more time working with your content and less time listening to you talking. More examples about course structure are included in the following five chapters.

Are you still unsure about how to proceed with your course redesign? Would you like to see some examples of redesigned courses? The following four chapters represent only a few of the myriad ways in which you can redesign your humanities course to improve student learning. The following courses were developed under the support and guidance of the University of North Texas's N-Gen Redesign Project™. Each faculty member leading the redesign effort received a $12,000 grant, which was used to buy a course release and to pay for graduate student assistance with content creation. The faculty member spent a year going through the process outlined in this book within a community of practice with other faculty members. The faculty met once each month to discuss specific topics (for example, how to write student learning outcomes or how to develop an assessment plan) and attended three full-day retreats. The faculty piloted the redesigned course the subsequent year and then made modifications based on the assessments. The N-Gen Redesign Project™ is supported by staff from the Center for Learning Enhancement, Assessment, and Redesign. You can follow the project at: http://qep.unt.edu and read the current cohort's blog at: http://ngenredesign.wordpress.com.

After reading this Chapter, you should have . . .
1. determined the teaching strategies you will use in the course.
2. completed the Instructional Activities Checklist.
3. aligned the teaching strategies with your Student Learning Outcomes.
4. aligned the teaching strategies with your Assessment Blueprint.
5. be prepared to pilot the teaching strategies with your students.

C   H   A   P   T   E   R   S   I   X

U.S. History I: Pre-Columbian through 1877

Dr. Kelly McMichael completed her Ph.D. in American History at the University of North Texas and has taught at several institutions including UNT, Texas Christian University, Dallas Baptist University, Florida Community College, Southeastern Community College—North Carolina, and the for-profit online Kaplan University, in addition to working in faculty professional development at the Center for Learning Enhancement, Assessment, and Redesign at the University of North Texas. McMichael was one of the first faculty members of the pilot that preceded the N-Gen project and began working in course redesign in 2004. She has been teaching and working in higher education for fifteen years.

What was this course like before you redesigned it?

This is a survey course required of all students in the state. It is traditionally taught using a lecture format with three or four non-comprehensive exams. Students have few opportunities to engage directly with the content, primary sources, each other, or the faculty member. At UNT, this course is taught in the large-enrollment format with between 125 and 300 students in each section.

How has it changed as a result of the redesign?

I spent an entire year redesigning this course and developing the curriculum materials, and I had three primary objectives when I began the N-Gen redesign process:
1. Students will learn the basic facts and chronology of U.S. History.
2. Students will engage directly with primary sources, applying them to solve historical problems in a real-world and relevant context.

3. Students' interest and motivation in U.S. History will increase, and they will become life-long learners of history.

It seemed to me that the course had stressed facts and chronology at the expense of application, giving students a false sense of what historians actually do. I wanted to correct this by emphasizing the interpretative nature of the discipline. I knew that to achieve this goal, I would have to find specific historical problems for the students to engage in that would hold their interest, but also serve as microcosms for the broader themes they needed to learn.

To meet these main objectives, the redesigned course has a two-part format:
1. <u>Students learn the facts and chronology of U.S. History through interactive, media-rich online lessons.</u> Each lesson is based on mastery learning so that students cannot move to the next lesson until they have achieved a faculty-set standard. Online content includes a comprehensive midterm and final exam.
2. <u>Students engage directly with primary sources, applying them to solve historical problems in a real-world and relevant context.</u> Students work on case studies (implemented as role-playing simulation games) that highlight specific historical content in a problem-based format.

The students work on the online portion of the class independently on their own and come to class to engage in the role-playing simulations. I believe this format gives them both a broad overview of the time period, which is what they normally receive in the survey, but also provides them with an in-depth exploration into particular topics. Students are rarely afforded a deep look at a historical situation in the survey course because there are always too many topics to cover. I "bought" time for a deep probe by eliminating the lecture component and replacing it with online materials.

Examples of Course Materials

The online course materials consist of 15 media-rich lessons anchored by a mastery-based quiz. Each lesson contains text, images, video, audio, and flash-based learning objects created in an attempt to address varying student learning styles.

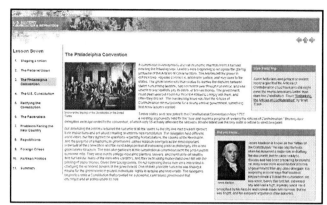

The lessons include:
- **Unit 1** Colliding Cultures
    Lesson 1: Pre-Columbian America
    Lesson 2: European Exploration and Colonization of the New World
    Lesson 3: The New World and the Old
    Lesson 4: The Colonial Experiment
- **Unit 2** Colonization and Revolution
    Lesson 5: The English Empire
    Lesson 6: The Revolution
    Lesson 7: Creating the United States
    Lesson 8: Change of Power
- **Unit 3** A New Nation Emerging
    Lesson 9: The Growing Nation
    Lesson 10: Rise in Democracy
    Lesson 11: American Society and Culture
    Lesson 12: Manifest Destiny
- **Unit 4** A Country Dividing
    Lesson 13: A House Dividing
    Lesson 14: Civil War
    Lesson 15: Reconstruction

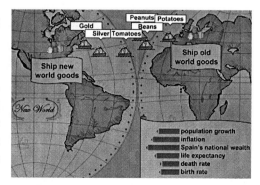

The in-class portion of the course consists of role-playing simulations played by the students. I generally use four simulations—one to anchor each of the course units. This is the heart of the class and reflects the "active learning" portion of the course. The simulations I have used that students like best are:

- CSI: Philip Nolan
- La Amistad: Revolt for Freedom
- The Politics of Manifest Destiny
- The Texas Troubles

The students are assigned specific roles to play in the simulations, are then divided into factions based on those roles so that they can work collaboratively, use primary source documents from which to prepare for their roles, and work outside of class within their factions in preparation for the in-class role-playing.

For example, the case study "The Politics of Manifest Destiny," is based on the counter-factual premise that the popularly-elected Texas Constitutional Convention, along with specific guests, gathered in June of 1845 to vote on two specific issues:

- to accept an offer of peace from the Mexican government, possibly ending hostilities between the two nations, or
- to accept an annexation proposal from the United States, bringing an end to the Republic of Texas.

The "guests" joining the convention members include former Texas Presidents Sam Houston and Mirabeau Lamar, Benjamin Lundy, Ashbel Smith, John Tyler, James K. Polk, Felix Huston, and a Comanche Chief. In reality, the Convention gathered to consider the proposal of annexation put forward by the United States, as well as a proposed peace treaty with Mexico. Once the convention accepted the annexation proposal, the proposal moved on to a popular vote held in October 1845. The game eliminates the popular vote and assumes that the members of the Constitutional Convention were representing specific constituents, had the power to vote on the two bills proposed, and that the vote would determine the legal outcome.

Students are given specific roles to play. There are nine roles that represent the key issues involved in making the decision to either vote for or against annexation. These roles represent the key players in the game. All other students play "indeterminates." The indeterminates are students who have primary and secondary objectives but who are undecided on the issue of annexation.

The active role-playing aspects of this simulation take place at the Caucus and Convention session. As President of the Republic of Texas, the student-playing Anson Jones runs the Caucus and Convention session. Jones calls for the caucuses to convene and organizes the format of the session. While Jones establishes the general rules of the proceedings, he also must decide how he will vote, along with the other indeterminates. The game facilitator (the instructor) informs Jones of his responsibilities and then allows him to take control of the proceedings.

The instructor (called the game facilitator during the role-playing portion of the simulation) organizes the game by dividing the students into their roles and providing a mini-lecture to ground the game in its period, providing background and context for the students.

The instructor establishes the game rules (assignments, due dates, discussion boards) and assists the students in preparing for the caucus and convention sessions. The instructor may also allow some in-class time for students to organize themselves.

During the caucus and convention session, the instructor literally and figuratively moves to the side. Anson Jones runs the class, determining the order of the caucus activities and session, and makes all major decisions. The students may call upon the instructor to clarify a fact. The instructor can insert a comment, but should keep it brief so that the students remain in control.

Once the role-playing simulation process has finished, the instructor holds a reflection session. During this time, the instructor briefs the students about what actually happened in the past and illustrates how the students' decisions and arguments were different from the ones actually made. The instructor encourages students to talk about their roles and the parts that they played, making the "larger" connections to the broad scope of United States History. They also discuss how their engagement in the simulation illustrates the interpretive nature of the discipline. Most students find it difficult to understand that History is not a series of names, dates, or "right" answers. The reflective session provides a perfect opportunity for the instructor to get into this higher-order thinking element.

The students are graded individually for their work in the role-playing simulation even though they work collaboratively during the preparation and play time. Each student writes two papers: one is a speech to be delivered at either the caucus or the convention and the other is a reflective paper completed at the end of the course. In addition to the two papers, each student is required to post materials online in their factions. These postings might include speeches, primary documents, thoughts, or strategies. The online postings have varied but have most often been on the discussion board of a learning management system, on a wiki, or on an open-sourced social networking site. The final component of a student's grade is oral performance. Because these case studies are conducted as role-playing simulations, the students are speaking in public. Each student receives an oral performance grade, based mostly on participation and preparation. See assessment examples below for rubrics used to grade the case studies.

Redesigned Course Structure

The greatest challenge I faced in implementing problem-based learning in my course involved the sheer number of students in a single class section. I knew that I needed to break the students into small groups and meet with the groups individually, but that is a challenge when there is only one instructor and one teaching assistant.

The first semester that I taught the redesigned course I had 125 students, and I broke them into five groups of 25 students. The student groups rotated into class once every two weeks to engage in the role-playing simulations. I was in the classroom on Monday, Wednesday, and Friday, but each group was assigned a "class day" and only came to class the one time, every other week. While this system allowed me to meet with each small group individually, it proved inadequate because two-week intervals between face-to-face meetings caused the students to lose momentum in the role-playing simulations.

Since the initial semester, I have changed the format so that each group of students comes to class once a week. This has improved the feelings of cohesiveness within the simulations and has given the course greater unity. I have accomplished this by training the teaching assistant to facilitate small groups, allowing for more than one group to meet at a time.

I have since modified the course structure so that an even larger section of students can be taught using this method. This is an example of human resource reallocation within the college paradigm. For example, in this format, 220 students have enrolled in the course section with one instructor of record. The students were then broken into 11 small groups with 20 students in each group. The instructor of record served as a course manager and trained six teaching assistants to facilitate the small group role-playing simulations. Each facilitator had a grader who graded all written assignments based on rubrics. The instructor trained the facilitators and graders, insured quality in the online component, and observed the facilitators during the in-class role-playing simulations.

Why would you (or your institution) consider reordering the ways in which people work in your department? There are many reasons why institutions are looking to reallocate human resources. These include costs, physical space limitations, and the increases in the numbers of students that must be served.

Although not yet tested, I projected this pedagogical approach to include up to 2,000 students in one section. The following flow chart illustrates what the human resource dynamic would look like using this structure.

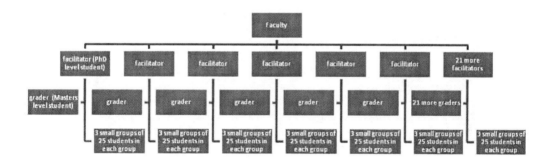

Despite the large number of students enrolled in the course, the students knew only that they met in groups of 20. They received a high degree of instructor-to-student and student to student contact during the semester, eliminating the anonymity often associated with large classes. Additionally, the cost per successful student makes this model extremely cost effective, despite the fact that there are far more individuals involved in the instructional delivery.

Sample of Student Learning Outcomes
UNIT ONE

STANDARD 1
Comparative characteristics of societies in the Americas, Western Europe, and Western Africa that increasingly interacted after 1450.

Standard 1A
The student understands the patterns of change in indigenous societies in the Americas prior to extensive European contact by the following means:

- Drawing upon data to identify, explain, and analyze the origins and migration from Asia to the Americas and contrasting them with Native Americans' own beliefs concerning their origins in the Americas **[maps, graphs, charts]**
- Knowledge, comprehension, analysis

- Identifying and explaining the rise and decline of the Mississippian mound-building and Aztec societies
- Knowledge, comprehension

Standard 1B
The student understands changes in Western European societies in the age of exploration by the following means:

- Identifying dissent within the Catholic Church, comparing and analyzing the beliefs and ideas of leading religious reformers. [**Explain the influence of ideas**]
- Knowledge, comprehension, analysis

- Identifying and analyzing relationships among the rise of centralized states, the development of urban centers, the expansion of commerce, and overseas exploration. [**Identify historical antecedents**]
- Knowledge, analysis

Standard 1C
The student understands developments in Western African societies in the period of early contact with Europeans by the following means:

- Identifying, comparing and analyzing varieties of slavery in Western Africa and the economic importance of the trans-Saharan slave trade in the 15th and 16th cen-

turies. [**Analyze multiple causation**]
- Knowledge, comprehension, analysis

- Identifying, comparing, and analyzing the varying responses of African states to early European trading and raiding on the Atlantic African coast. [**Analyze cause-and-effect relationships**]
- Knowledge, comprehension, analysis

Standard 1D
The student understands the differences and similarities among Africans, Europeans, and Native Americans who converged in the western hemisphere after 1492 by the following means:

- Identifying and comparing political systems, including concepts of political authority, civic values, and the organization and practice of government. [**Compare and contrast different political systems**]
- Knowledge, comprehension

- Identifying and comparing social organizations, including population levels, urbanization, family structure, and modes of communication. [**Compare and contrast different social organizations**]
- Knowledge, comprehension

- Identifying and comparing economic systems, including systems of labor, trade, concepts of property, and exploitation of natural resources. [**Compare and contrast different economic institutions**]
- Knowledge, comprehension

- Identifying and comparing dominant ideas and values including religious belief and practice, gender roles, and attitudes toward nature. [**Compare and contrast the influence of ideas**]
- Knowledge, comprehension

STANDARD 2
How early European exploration and colonization resulted in cultural and ecological interactions among previously unconnected peoples.

Standard 2A
The student understands the stages of European oceanic and overland exploration, amid international rivalries, from the 9th to 17th centuries by the following means:

- Identifying and analyzing routes taken by early explorers, from the 15th through the 17th century, around Africa, to the Americas, and across the Pacific. [**Draw upon data in historical maps**]
- Knowledge, analysis

- Determining and evaluating the significance of Columbus' voyages and his interactions with indigenous peoples. [**Assess the importance of the individual in history**]
- Analysis, evaluation

- Comparing and making generalizations about the English, French, and Dutch motives for exploration with those of the Spanish. [**Compare and contrast different sets of ideas**]
- Comprehension, analysis, synthesis,

- Identifying, analyzing and evaluating the course and consequences of the "Columbian Exchange." [**Hypothesize the influence of the past**]
- Knowledge, analysis, evaluation

Standard 2B
The student understands the Spanish and Portuguese conquest of the Americas by the following means:

- Describing the social composition of the early settlers and comparing their various motives for exploration and colonization. [**Compare and contrast differing sets of ideas**]
- Comprehension, analysis

- Comparing and evaluating the Spanish interactions with such people as Aztecs, Incas, and Pueblos. [**Examine the influence of ideas**]
- Comprehension, analysis, evaluation

- Describing and comparing the evolution and long-term consequences of labor systems such as encomienda and slavery in Spanish and Portuguese America. [**Appreciate historical perspectives**]
- Comprehension, analysis

Sample of Assessment Plan

UNIT 1		Item Difficulty				
			Cognitive Levels			
		Low	Medium	High		
Supporting Objectives / Cognitive category	Learning Outcomes	Literal/Factual/Recall	Interpretive/Inferential	Critical-thinking/Evaluative	Items per outcome	Items per concept
Goal 1						
Obj. 1	Outcome 1	1	0	0	1	
	Outcome 2	4	0	0	4	5
Obj. 2	Outcome 1	1	0	0	1	
	Outcome 2	1	0	0	1	2
Obj. 3	Outcome 1		0	1	1	1
Obj. 4	Outcome 1	1	0	0	1	
	Outcome 2	0	0	0	0	1
Goal 2						
Obj. 1	Outcome 1	0	2	0	2	
	Outcome 2	0	1	1	2	
	Outcome 3	1	2	0	3	
	Outcome 4	1	1	0	2	9
Obj. 2	Outcome 1	3	0	0	3	
	Outcome 2	1	4	0	5	8

Course Effectiveness

The following data is taken from a Fall 2007 pilot of the course materials at the University of North Texas. The same instructor taught the pilot of the course and the control group (comparison class). I was not the instructor in these courses, meaning that we wanted to see how effective someone else could be teaching with this pedagogical approach.

U.S. History I:

Enrollment: 212 pilot versus 122 comparative
Completion: 208 pilot versus 118 comparative
> *Success Rates in two courses taught by same instructor*

Pilot Course: 87%
Traditional Course: 56%
> *Failure rates in two courses taught by same instructor*

Pilot Course: 13%
Traditional Course: 44%
> *Success rates of pilot compared with ALL large enrollment (150+) sections taught at UNT:*

Pilot Course: 87%
Traditional Course: 64%
> *Percent students who preferred the redesign format over traditional Lecture in U.S. History 1301*

Pilot Course: 57%
Traditional Course: 39%

Success Rates for Redesign versus average of UNT sections with more than 150 students

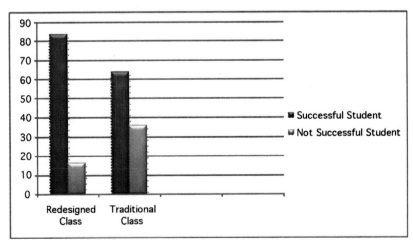

Highly Successful Rates:
UNT Students Highly Successful in Redesign Course as compared with a
Traditional Course taught by same faculty member

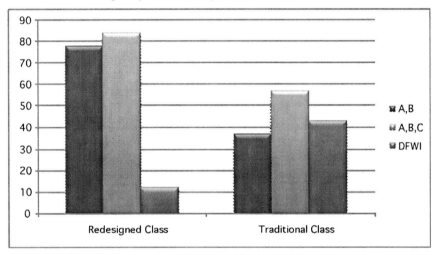

Student Reaction to the Redesigned Course

The following are student comments from a survey taken mid-semester about the
course pedagogical approach:

"At first when I found out what this class was I was a little upset and annoyed
because I felt confused by the first game and I felt it would be easier to just
listen to a lecture and take notes. True it might have been easier to listen (or
day dream) through a lecture, but would I have learned as much? In reality I
probably did learn more through the mixed course than I would've memorizing facts for a test that I would have forgotten the next day anyway. This class
proved a fun and entertaining way to learn. The papers were a bit of a hassle
at times, but I got them done. I always forgot about the quizzes though. There
should be more in-class reminders on those."

"I would prefer a face-to-face format because I am the type of person who
needs set rules and regulations. With taking quizzes and writing papers and
posting discussions online, I constantly forget to do them because I am not
used to doing everything on the internet. Whenever we do not have class
time, I consider that time free time and not time to do work."

"N-Gen Redesign. I think it worked better/easier for interaction. Face to face
class tends to be boring and being able to do most of the work online saves

time and makes it easier for me to learn. I feel I actually learn more rather than just memorizing information for a test."

Unexpected Benefits

I benefited in many unexpected ways from becoming involved in course redesign. Primarily, I think, by a reinvigoration of my teaching. I had taught the U.S. Survey for many years, sometimes teaching the same class four times in a single semester. The content and the process of teaching had become stale, and there were days that I simply dreaded going to class. I was usually ok after I arrived and got started, but I knew that I couldn't keep teaching with that attitude indefinitely. Redesigning the course helped me to remember what I had loved about teaching and re-instilled in me that passion for my subject that sets apart the best learning experiences.

At UNT, the N-Gen Redesign process is undertaken within a larger community-of-practice and for the first time in my academic career, teaching took center stage. Once a month, I gathered with others from multiple disciplines undergoing the same process, and our meetings became hot-beds of imagination, creativity, and excitement. It was thrilling to learn that the techniques Biology professors use to teach could be modified and used in History or Art. Working with faculty across disciplines reinforced my belief that nothing should be taught to students out of context. A single three-credit-hour class might make sense in terms of book-keeping, but it makes no sense in terms of learning. Gather five professors from five different disciplines and inevitably they will discover that their content intersects in interesting and compelling ways. This emphasis on intersection is the way education should be delivered. While I can't single-handedly convince institutions to modify their core structures, I can do my part by pairing with other faculty to team-teach or to work collaboratively. Overall, this experience has encouraged me to continue to seek communities within my institution where I can work with others.

How can this course be modified or adopted by another instructor?

Other instructors could easily adapt the pedagogical approach that I took in this course. First, it is based on principles from mastery learning, meaning that students are allowed the time and practice needed to master a set of concepts before moving on to the next. I don't believe that students should be "punished" for not getting questions right on a quiz, rather, they should use that information to learn where they are lacking in skills or knowledge. Mastery learning allows students to learn at different speeds and without the negative connotations associated with the usual college assessment practices.

While the Humanities and Social Sciences have been slow to adapt to any pedagogical techniques other than lecture, case-based learning and role-playing simulations have been used with great effect by business and medical schools for decades. I didn't invent these techniques, I just applied them to a History class and discovered quickly that this approach not only made sense, but increased student understanding and enjoyment of the course materials dramatically.

Some faculty complain that there are not a readily available supply of case studies or role-playing simulations for use in the classroom, and they are correct. But institutions and companies are listening to instructors and are supplying these in greater numbers. Some are even available for free as a result of state and national grants. For example, there is an organization at UNT called the Active Learning Initiative that has received multiple grants to create educational games, including role-playing simulations. Some of their products are available to the public for free for use in the classroom, including some of the case studies I have mentioned above. See http://ali.unt.edu.

Finally, the human resource reallocation experiments used with this course are worthy of consideration and further exploration. Institutions must address the growing numbers of students, the physical space limitations, and the dynamics involved in large lecture sections. We must serve more students, but we are also obligated to ensure that we provide them with an educational experience that will prepare them for the future. How to accomplish these two goals forms the basis of the educational mandate for the next decade.

C   H   A   P   T   E   R   S   E   V   E   N

Music Appreciation

Cynthia Beard, PhD Candidate[1]

Cynthia Beard is completing a PhD in Musicology and has taught in higher educa-tion for four years. As an outgrowth of participating in the N-Gen Course Redesign™ project at UNT, she became involved in student retention and now leads the Student Intervention Project at UNT. The project began as an experimental study in intervention, triggered by student non-participation in course work, and has grown to a formal program developed to improve retention at the University.

What was this course like before you redesigned it?

Students take this course to complete their fine arts credit, and they seem to like the course. Most have some experience with music—they've played in the high school band, have taken music lessons, or simply love music. Because they like music, they are fairly motivated when they come to class, but the format seems to impinge on that natural love. The class is generally taught face-to-face using lecture to a class section of 220 students. Music samples are played in class, but mostly the instructor talks about the music while the students sit passively. Students did not read the assigned textbook materials and did not come to class prepared. Fundamentally the course con-sisted of reading a textbook, listening to the accompanying CD of music, then com-ing to class and listening to the instructor point out the most significant historical and stylistic points related to the music. Exams were given to test students' factual knowl-edge, as well as their ability to identify and situate the music assigned for listening.

How has it changed as a result of the redesign?

This course has moved from a face-to-face lecture format to a blended class where most of the content (the lecture material) has been moved online. The time that the students are in-class has become something more like a laboratory environment. Three small discussion groups of 25 students each meet once a week most weeks and then the entire class meets together an average of eighteen days during the semester. These large section class meetings feature specialized lectures that draw on the expertise of guest lecturers—most of whom are musicians—for the purpose of holding live music demonstrations.   Some of the goals for the course include:

- The mastery of basic terminology used to discuss music
- The ability to place specific musical compositions into history style periods, genres, and a composers' output
- Developing listening skills:
    - Aural recognition of the salient features in assigned pieces
    - Aural recognition of similar features in other musical selections in non-assigned pieces
- Development of critical thinking:
    - Assessment of what we individually and socially value in music and what was valued during the major historical style periods
    - Analysis of a musical opinion for its strengths and weaknesses
- The ability to communicate ideas and information about music in coherent written prose.

Examples of Course Materials

The **online component** of the course consists of 25 multi-media lessons that emphasize musical style across four main periods: Baroque, Classical, Romantic, and 20th Century. The goal for the course is for students to be able to understand music stylistically rather than for them to be able to identify and classify musicians and music styles.

The online content includes multiple flash-based learning objects that assist students with analyzing musical style. The students can practice with the music clips as often as they need to be able to identify one style as compared with another.

Other learning objects are included in the content that help students learn how music is composed. For example, the following illustration is taken from a learning object that teaches students how Bach's Fugue No. 2 in C minor is constructed.

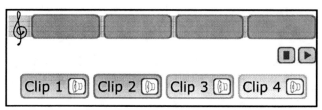

The interaction teaches students about the way that fugues are constructed. A fugue typically begins with a single line of music (one pitch at a time), with no accompaniment. Then the line is imitated (or copied) at a different pitch level, at the same time that another musical idea is played. The effect is that a fugue will have multiple lines of music sounding simultaneously, which creates a complex relationship between the pitches. When music is put together in this manner, it is called "polyphonic."

Fugues are quite different from most of the music we encounter today. We are accustomed to hearing music with just one melody and an accompaniment, but during Bach's lifetime, audiences were familiar with fugues and other types of polyphonic music. After students have read the online lesson on Bach's fugues and worked with this interaction, they will have a better understanding of the way that Baroque music was composed.

To use this interaction, students drag the numbered clips on to the musical staff in a random order. The "play" button allows the fragments of music that are attached to the clips to be played in the order that the student has created, enabling students to "compose" their own musical example. In addition to creating a randomized arrangement, students may also attempt to place the clips into Bach's order, based on what they have heard. When the clips are out of order, the "correct" beginning of the fugue becomes more obvious because it will sound out of place.

The first section (called the Exposition) of Bach's Fugue No. 2 in C minor, from Well-tempered Clavier, Book 1, is used in this interaction.

The **face-to-face classroom sessions** are divided into two different types:
- Large lecture meetings, including course orientation at the beginning of the semester and guest musical performances throughout the term, and
- Small discussion groups, with approximately twenty-five students at a time.

This second component, the small discussion meetings, is one of the most distinctive elements of the redesigned blended version of the course. In this small group setting, students are engaged in experiential learning activities that reinforce information from the online lessons.

Our most successful structure for the in-class activities involved debates in which the students were divided into two teams.

For example, one of the debates held grew out of the online lesson about the music of the Baroque composer Johann Sebastian Bach. Today, many people do not realize that

Bach was somewhat old-fashioned during the last years of his life, when other composers were beginning to explore a new, melodically driven Classical style. On the other hand, some individuals believed Bach's music to be overly complicated. During the debate, the students put Bach's music on trial by looking at it through a historical lens. Does Bach's music stand on it own? Is it outdated? The debate isn't about whether students like Bach, or not, but whether his music has stood the test of time.

Redesigned Course Structure

The redesigned course is taught using this structure:
- 18 large lecture meetings
- 5 small discussion group rotations
- Approximately 25 students in each group
- Facilitated by an instructor and two teaching assistants
- 25 online lessons
- The structure can also be understood in terms of approach to content. See the following visualization of the approach to content in the course.

Basic Diagram of Approach to the content in this Course

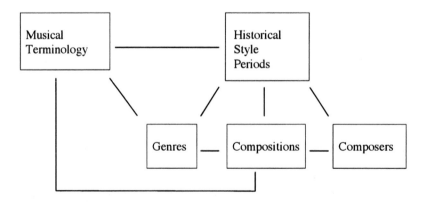

Constant Question: What do we value in music, and what has been valued historically?

Course Effectiveness

The course student success rate (as measured by As, Bs, and Cs) has continued to improve each semester that it has been taught using this format. Data from the pilot shows that as the instructor mastered the pedagogical approach, student success improved:

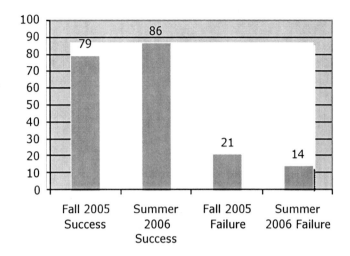

Student Reaction to the Redesigned Course

Student reaction to the course has been positive. See the following comments for examples of what students said about the course in a survey taken at the end:

> "I believe the mixed course is a wonderful idea and it works very well. Listening notebooks are a grand idea. Small groups are also a good idea. Allows for a comfortable atmosphere. Can't imagine the course any different. I learned a lot."

> "I believe the mixed course is a wonderful idea and it works very well."
> "Small groups are also a good idea. Allows for a comfortable atmosphere."

> "Can't imagine the course any different. I learned a lot."

Unexpected Benefits

Redesigning the course resulted in several different kinds of benefits. The course achieved a new level of learning not previously experienced. The students were not just engaged in rote memorization, but were thinking deeply about music and then applying the analysis they had learned while studying Bach to the Beastie Boys (and all the kinds of music that they loved).

And for the first time, the students were actually being assessed on what I wanted them to learn and experience—higher order thinking skills.

How can this course be modified or adopted by another instructor?

Another instructor could easily adapt the pedagogical approach of this course. The lessons developed were modular in nature and were used to eliminate the need for lengthy lectures and to appeal to students with varying learning styles. Because the course aim became teaching students to analyze and assess musical styles, the online format allowed them to practice those skills repeatedly until they had mastered them.

The in-class activities turned out to be the most meaningful contact hours for the students and it was in these debates and discussions that students began to be able to connect the music that they were learning about to the larger social and cultural issues around them—in the past, present, and potentially into the future. An instructor could take this approach for a blended class with problem-based learning at its core and reproduce it to meet their students' needs and the instructor's research expertise.

C H A P T E R   E I G H T

Art Survey II: Art History from 1400 to 2008

Dr. Kelly Donahue-Wallace and Dr. Denise Baxter[1]

Kelly Donahue-Wallace is an associate professor of art history and the Chair of Art Education and Art History at UNT. Dr. Donahue-Wallace's field of expertise is Latin American Art, European Renaissance and Baroque Art, and Print History. Her PhD is from the University of New Mexico. Denise Baxter is an assistant professor of Art History at UNT. She completed her PhD at the University of California at Santa Barbara with an expertise in Eighteenth and Nineteenth-Century European Art.

What was this course like before you redesigned it?

This course addresses painting, sculpture, and architecture from Europe, the United States, and selected non-Western cultures between 1400 and the present. The course serves 315 students every spring semester. The majority of the students who take this course come from the College of Visual Arts and Design. The course satisfies the Visual and Performing Art core curriculum requirement and usually meets on a Monday, Wednesday, Friday schedule with one professor and three teaching assistants, each employed at 25 percent time. The course is taught using lecture with three or four exams and two or three papers. Although concepts are stressed in the lecture, the assignments and exams privilege recall over critical thinking. Additionally, the students completing this course arrive in the upper level courses without the content knowledge or the critical thinking skills needed to succeed.

How has this course changed as a result of the redesign?

Traditionally this course is taught as an overview that includes as many examples as possible of art, sculpture, and architecture from the period. The newly designed course focuses on art history methodology rather than the memorization of a cannon of art. To achieve this focus, the course has been divided into seven units representing the major artistic periods between 1400 and 2008. Each period is anchored by a single, representative piece of art, sculpture, or architecture. The entire unit revolves around this single piece of art as students learn to "read" the art based on a corresponding methodological approach. Other pieces of art, sculpture, or architecture enhance or contrast the single piece of representative art.

The Redesigned Course Structure

The redesigned course is still delivered on a Monday, Wednesday, Friday schedule to 300 plus students, but the new format has all the students attending a lecture on Mondays and once more during the next two-week cycle. Students attend the second day as part of a small group of 20, using the time when they are not in class to solve problem-based learning challenges. See the following chart for what the class structure looks like:

Art History Structure using Two-Week Cycles

		Monday	Wednesday	Friday
	Wk 1	Everyone in class for lecture	Everyone in class for lecture	Everyone in class for lecture
Unit 1	Wk 2	Everyone in-class for lecture	Groups A, B, C, D	Groups E, F, G, H
	Wk3	Everyone in-class for lecture	Groups I, J, K, L	Groups M, N, O, P
Unit 2	Wk 4	Everyone in-class for lecture	Groups A, B, C, D	Groups E, F, G, H
	Wk 5	Everyone in-class for lecture	Groups I, J, K, L	Groups M, N, O, P

Examples of Course Materials

The seven problem-based learning challenges with "real life" scenarios form the core of this course. These challenges are augmented with scholarly readings, reviews, and interviews. The course no longer requires a textbook. In addition to the readings, the students work directly with objects and monuments from local public and museum collections and each other in small-group discussions.

The seven problems used in the course correspond with the seven course units and are matched with a specific methodological approach:

- Renaissance: Formalism and Iconography
- Baroque/Rococo: Space
- Neoclassicism: Public Sphere
- Realism/Impressionism: Commodity/Marxism
- Cubism: Towards Abstraction: The "Other"
- Abstract Expressionism: Cult of the Artist
- Postmodernism: Postmodernism

For every two-week module, the students are required to:

- Attend two lectures
- Attend one discussion section
- Read scholarly texts
- Answer reading questions
- Solve a "problem"

All meetings, readings, discussions, and assignments are related the specific object being studied that is representative of the period. The object was chosen in light of the methodological approach being undertaken in the unit.

An online course shell houses the problems and additional materials used by the students. The images here represent the main page of the online portion of the class and a screen shot of a Flash learning object created about the Palace of Versailles.

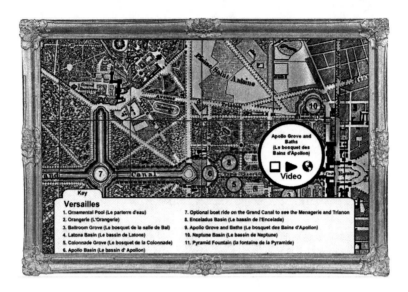

Sample of the "Problem" from the Lesson on Cubism

Cubism: Toward Abstraction II

Defining the "Other" in a DFW Museum[2]

The directors of several museums in the Dallas-Ft. Worth area have completed the readings for this unit and viewed the video of Edward Said. During a conference call, they determined that there were many works in the museums' collections that participated in this misrepresentation of Others: women and non-White peoples (Africans, Asians, Native Americans, Latin American Indians, etc.). They decided that the best way to begin the process of addressing this in their presentations of museum content was to have students from UNT review their collections and exhibitions. They want the students to problematize (meaning to raise critical questions about) the appropriation of non-Western forms and the representation of women and people of color at the local museums.

The museums participating in this critical evaluation are:

Dallas Museum of Art
Kimbell Art Museum
Meadows Museum
Amon Carter Museum
Fort Worth Modern Art Museum

So, the directors have hired you to do the work! You will write a 750-word critical evaluation of the representation of the Other at one of the area museums.

Instructions:
- Choose one of the museums listed above. You must visit the museum. This assignment cannot be completed by looking at the museums' websites.
- Visit the museum and examine how objects on display made between 1800 and 1950 represent Others (women and non-White peoples) in light of the readings you completed for this unit.
- Your essay will have an Introduction, three sections (in three or more paragraphs), and a Conclusion. Insert a hard return between each paragraph. Spell check before submitting.
- Your Introduction will state your thesis. The thesis must articulate your evaluation of the museum's treatment of the Other.
- In the first section, you will write specifically about at least one European or US object made between 1800 and 1950 that presents an image of women that reflects Carol Duncan's essay. Describe what the object represents and analyze the image using Duncan's thesis.
- In the second section, you will write specifically about a European or US object made between 1800 and 1950 representing non-White peoples. Describe what the object represents and explain how Leighten's and Said's arguments are confirmed by the object.
- The final part of the critical evaluation will summarize the overall treatment of the Other at the museum. Address the percentage of displayed works that construct an image of the Other. Also identify the array of Others represented in the collection of 1800-1950 US and European works.
- The Conclusion will summarize how the paper has argued your thesis.

Be sure to employ relevant terms and concepts in your essays. You also need to use your best writing, grammar, spelling, and punctuation.

Let's get started.
Cubism: Resources

What will I need to solve the Problem?

Use these resources to solve the Problem.

Lecture notes:
Be sure to take careful notes during the two lectures in this module. You should also refer to your notes from 1800 on. Pay attention to how both form and content engage questions of the Other.

Readings:
The readings you do for the discussion section will also be necessary for solving the Problem.

Discussion Board:
Although you are not required to use the discussion board, it always helps to discuss ideas with classmates. Ask your questions there. Seek advice.

Additional websites:
Orientalist Art of the Nineteenth Century, http://www.orientalistart.net/
Japonisme from the Metropolitan Museum of Art,
        http://www.metmuseum.org/toah/hd/jpon/hd_jpon.htm
Japanese prints from the Metropolitan Museum of Art,
        http://www.metmuseum.org/toah/hd/ukiy/hd_ukiy.htm
A commercial site on Picasso and African art,
        http://www.drloriv.com/lectures/african.asp
Orientalism in Nineteenth-Century Art from the Metropolitan Museum of Art,
        www.metmuseum.org/toah/hd/euor/hd_euor.htm
Conserving Le Demoiselles d'Avignon from the Modern Art Museum of New York,
        www.moma.org/collection/conservation/demoiselles/index.html

Cubism: Completing the Problem
Once you have visited the museum and prepared your critical evaluation, it is time to turn in the work.
• Go to the Assignment Turn-In Application (ATA) page. Log in with your EUID and Password. Choose ART2360.1.
• In the ATA, click Assignments and select Towards Abstraction. This will take you to the Description page. The Description shows you the question you will answer and the number of images you will need for this assignment (none).
• Click the Questions tab. This is will bring you to the page where you will paste in your critical evaluation. Be sure to click the Save button as you go.
• When you have finished entering your answers click Submit Assignment.

Helpful Hints:

Compose your answers in a word processing program then copy and paste into the answer boxes. This will allow you to run spell-check. It will also let you save your answers as a back up!

Remember to compose your written submissions in your best writing, with proper punctuation, capitalization, and grammar. Our inclination online is to do things short-hand. Keep in mind that this is still a college course!

How Will This Problem Be Graded?

Your reports will be graded using the following rubric.

Student...	1 Poor	2	3 Average	4	5 Excellent
...selected an example that supports Duncan's thesis					
...correctly applied Duncan's thesis ...selected an example that supports Leighten's and Said's theses					
...correctly applied Leighten's and Said's theses					
...correctly evaluated the museum's representation of the Other					
...employed appropriate vocabulary					
Total points					

Point Scale:
A= 27-30= 90-100%
B= 24-26= 80-89%
C= 21-23= 70-79%
D= 18-20= 60-69%
F= 17 and below= 59% or less

Explanation of values in the sample rubric:

Explanation/Analysis/Comparison
- Excellent answer will reflect correct and complete knowledge/analysis of the ideas.
- Average answer will reflect some but not all of the ideas.
- Poor answer will have little correct information about the ideas.

Use of relevant terminology
- Excellent answers use all of the relevant terms possible. These are the standard terms of arts disciplines and communicate ideas of form, content, material, and context.
- Average answers have some terms and concepts, but several key terms are missing.
- Poor answers include few terms and concepts.

Sample of Course Student Learning Outcomes

Core Curriculum Outcomes (CCO)
- Demonstrate awareness of the scope and variety of works of art.
- Understand those works as expressions of individual and human values within an historical and social context.
- Demonstrate knowledge of the influence of literature, philosophy, and/or the arts on intercultural experiences.
- Develop an appreciation for the aesthetic principles that guide or govern the artistic production within discrete periods and eras.

Department Outcomes (DO)
- Employ the specialized vocabulary of the discipline of art history.
- Identify key objects and monuments within a breadth of discrete periods and regions of artistic production.
- Demonstrate knowledge of the history and literature of methodologies employed in art history.

Course Outcomes (CO)
- Perform formal, iconographic, and functional analyses of objects and monuments within their social and historical contexts.
- Demonstrate knowledge of several methodologies employed by art historians.
- Apply the appropriate method to the discussion of an object or monument.
- Employ the vocabulary specific to the visual arts and the discipline of art history.
- Identify an array of objects and monuments created between 1300 and 2000.

- Compare the general formal, iconographic, and functional characteristics of the major artistic period styles from 1300-2000.
- Analyze the function and intention of art exhibitions.

Lesson Outcomes
One
- Analyze the formal characteristics of a work of art that employs Renaissance pictorial principles. (CO 1, 2, and 3)
- Analyze the iconographic characteristics of a work of art that employs narrative. (CO 1, 2 and 3)
- Employ the terminology and concepts relevant to the art and architecture of the Italian Renaissance period. (DO 1, CO 4)
- Identify and compare a related object or monuments (CCO 1 and 4; DO 2; CO 5 and 6)

Two
- Analyze the formal, iconographic, and functional characteristics of an object and/or monument with Baroque and/or Rococo characteristics within its social and historical context. (CCO 2 and 3; CO 1, 2, and 3)
- Use social context and concepts of historicized lived experience as a methodology through which to interpret an object and/or monument with Baroque and/or Rococo characteristics (CCO 2 and 3; DO 3; CO 2, 3)
- Employ the terminology relevant to the art and architecture of the Baroque and Rococo styles. (DO 1, CO 4)
- Design a plan for a walking tour that employs the concepts relevant to a socio-historical methodology. (CCO 1, 2 and 3; DO 3; CO 2, 3, 5, 6, and 7)

Unexpected Benefits

There were several benefits derived from redesigning this course. For Dr. Baxter, these included:
- Actually getting to know the students in the course (little one-to-one interaction had been possible with over 300 students in a single section)
- Collaborating with masters-level graduate students to lead the small-group discussion actually taught these students how to teach the course
- Students seem to be retaining the information and the methodology after leaving the course

How can another instructor adopt this course?

Another instructor could adopt this course in whole, taking the same problems created by Donahue-Wallace and Baxter and reusing them or reusing the problem, replacing the art, architecture, or sculpture within the problem to ones local to the institution. More fundamentally, the general approach could be adapted easily as a means by which to structure the survey.

C H A P T E R   N I N E

Masterpieces of World Literature from the Ancients through the Early Renaissance

Dr. Tracey Gau[1]

Dr. Tracey Gau has a Ph.D. in Renaissance, Rhetoric, and Composition from Texas Christian University and became involved in UNT's N-Gen Course Redesign project in 2006. She has taught literature classes at UNT for ten years. Dr. Gau's emphasis is on teaching and she has become an expert on assessment at the course level.

What was this course like before you redesigned it?

At UNT, this class is part of the core curriculum, fulfilling the general humanities requirement. It is taught in sections that average between 60 and 150 students each. The class meets twice a week for lecture with three exams and ten one-page papers. The students are asked to read the assigned literature prior to class, but many do not. Attendance is often a problem, which is unfortunate since this class is one of the ways the department recruits for the major. The instructor didn't believe that the course was taught badly in the original format, she just didn't know what other pedagogical approaches were possible before becoming involved with the N-Gen Course Redesign™ project.

How has it changed as a result of the redesign?

It became apparent to the instructor that between the large numbers of students served in the literature courses and the high failure rates, a new method was needed for teaching these classes more productively. After the year-long redesign process, the World Literature class is taught using a blended format in such a way that "technology becomes an enabler to move students through a process of internalizing, experiencing, and relating to literature at the meta-cognitive level. Students attend both large-group, face-to-face lecture classes and small, cooperative-base group discussion sessions. Throughout, students progress through interactive online learning activities that move them from low-level learning objectives (literal and factual) to medium-level objectives that require interpretive and inferential work. Students use these cognitively rich online learning activities to self-assess how carefully they are mastering the content. In the small group meetings, students collaborate, debate, and present their own conclusions in the context of others'. To further meet high-level learning objectives that require evaluation and logic, students construct informed, organized, coherent written responses to the texts. This combination of face-to-face and online learning involves students in all facets of cognitive complexity in order to integrate a higher level of critical thinking into the course, to hone student-writing skills, and to improve success, retention, and motivation rates that are measured with reliability and validity."[2]

Examples of Course Materials

"The **online materials** in the course use technology to meet a variety of learning styles through visual, audio, and interactive content. In addition, low-stakes mastery quizzes and games, like the version of BINGO shown below, allow students to self-assess how carefully they are mastering the material at the conceptual level.

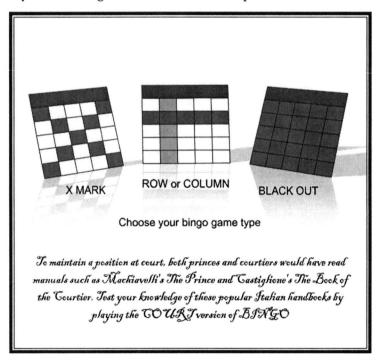

X MARK   ROW or COLUMN   BLACK OUT

Choose your bingo game type

To maintain a position at court, both princes and courtiers would have read manuals such as Machiavelli's The Prince and Castiglione's The Book of the Courtier. Test your knowledge of these popular Italian handbooks by playing the COURT version of BINGO

In this visually enhanced BINGO-style learning object, students engage in formative learning about concepts, characters, and cultural elements from both the Renaissance period and the Ancient world that helped to shape early-modern texts. This activity requires the application of new and previously studied concepts to the current texts. The online lessons were developed as preparatory and mastery components to lead the students through the literature through the use of fun activities. These activities help the students gain confidence with the basic characters and plots of the readings.

Each online lesson has specific outcomes (displayed to the student on the first page of the lesson) to which activities are tied. The activities are aimed at low and medium cognitive level outcomes to insure mastery of the rote materials. The lessons have been developed to appeal to a variety of learning styles.

The **face-to-face classroom** activities are experientially based and are conducted in small, stable cooperative groups that foster a high level of preparedness, facilitate more active and consistent participation in discussion and problem-solving, and promote independent thinking by making students accountable for important aspects of their learning.

In one group activity, students debate whether Shakespeare was indeed the author of the famous plays or whether other contemporary figures from the period may be viable candidates for authorship. Students read a set of current articles about the authorship controversy in order to prepare for a small-group class debate. When they arrive to class, each small group is given a particular theory of authorship that they must defend and support, forming their own conclusions at the end of the period based on the evidence and arguments presented in-class."[3]

Redesigned Course Structure

The redesigned course retained a lecture component. The instructor lectures to the entire section once every two weeks and in the interim, smaller groups of 50 students rotate through the course. The smaller groups of 50 are divided further into stable sub-groups of 10 students.

Previously the instructor believed she had taught to the most basic understanding of the literature, but the redesigned format has allowed her to teach to the top. Not only can she be sure that they have mastered the factual, literal level but she has now had time to model the analytical process involved in breaking literature down and fitting it back together. She has time to show students how the literature is inevitably tied with the life and culture of the times in which it was written. "It's the learning of process that becomes meaningful to the students," said Gau.

The overall course has been designed to be recursive, "allowing students to be assessed formatively before they are evaluated summatively." Additionally, the course structure and materials offer a high degree of flexibility to the student, letting them control their own learning environment to a far greater extent than usual. The group work serves multiple purposes but in particular models the idea that none of us learn in a vacuum. We learn "socially."

Sample of Student Learning Outcomes

The following represents the student learning outcomes for the course:
I.   Demonstrate an awareness and recognition of the scope and variety of works of literature
     a. Recall and recognize the historical sequence of major literary figures, texts, and movements within the Ancient, Middle, and Renaissance periods
     b. Identify conventional literary genres, elements, and devices
     c. Employ discipline specific vocabulary in order to recognize the relationship between form and content
     d. Relate literary or cultural concepts, principles, terms, strategies, and styles to a range of literature
II. Read critically and analytically
     a. Analyze, evaluate, interpret, and synthesize representative texts from the Eastern and Western traditions and relate them to their literary and cultural contexts
     b. Compare and contrast major literary figures, their situations, and decisions
     c. Make connections among various periods, texts, authors, and characters
     d. Evaluate the ideas presented in a text, their implications, and their relationship to ideas beyond the text
III. Construct informed, organized, and coherent written responses to literary texts
     a. Formulate a central interpretive idea about the texts
     b. Develop ideas logically and coherently with adequate supporting textual examples
     c. Present ideas clearly and concisely
     d. Observe the standard conventions of formatting, citation, grammar, and punctuation
IV. Actively discuss ideas with others
     a. Present (in discussion posts and/or small groups) information or conclusions that help other students summarize, synthesize, and integrate the conceptual material
     b. Establish a relevancy between literature and how it affects one's life, personal values, ethical behavior, aesthetic judgment, and problem solving

Sample of a Rubric Used in the Course

Scoring Rubric for SLO #3:
Construct an informed, organized, and coherent written response to the literary text

Dimension	5	10	15	20	Tot
THESIS A debatable, problematic assertion	An attempt at an assertion is made, but it is not problematic; discussion is mostly summary	Assertion is obvious and contributes little to the on-going discussion	Assertion is interpretive and moderately contributes to the on-going discussion	Assertion is interpretive, problematic, and clearly contributes to the on-going discussion	
EVIDENCE Substantiate the assertion	The relationship between the examples and the assertion is unclear	Examples are not clearly or consistently linked to the assertion	Examples moderately support and are relevant to the assertion	Examples clearly support and are relevant to the assertion	
ORGANI-ZATION Coherent structure	The assertion is not logically maintained throughout the paper, and relationships between ideas are unclear	The assertion is logically maintained to a moderate degree; supporting statements are weak in connecting to the original assertion	The assertion is logically maintained throughout, and supporting statements are moderately consistent in referring to the original assertion	The assertion is logically maintained throughout, and supporting statements are highly consistent in referring to the original assertion	
SIGNIF-ICANCE Establish a relevancy	Conclusion merely summarizes the assertion attempt	Significance or relevancy is implied but not clearly conveyed	Conclusion moderately conveys the significance or relevancy of the assertion	Conclusion clearly conveys the significance or relevancy of the assertion	
©2008 T.M.Gau					
Mechanics	**0**	**5**	**10**		
Grammar, sentence structure, punctuation	Inaccuracies make paper difficult to read	Inaccuracies make paper moderately difficult to read	Few inaccuracies, advanced vocabulary, deliberate word choice	N/A	
Quotations	Inaccurately cited or integrated	Accurately cited and integrated	N/A	N/A	
Format	Does not meet MLA standards: format, heading, spacing, margins, and title	Meets MLA standards: format, heading, spacing, margins, and title	N/A	N/A	

Grand Total ___

Feedback:

Sample of the Course Assessment Plan

©2008 T.M.Gau — Assessment Plan for N-Gen ENGL2210: World Literature I — Dr. Tracey Gau

Domain	Course Learning Goals (Institutional)	General Student Learning Outcomes (Departmental)	Specific Lesson Learning Outcomes (Classroom)	Low	Med	High	Tot	CR
World Literature – Ancient through Renaissance	Demonstrate an awareness and recognition of the scope and variety of works of literature	Recall and recognize the historical sequence of major literary figures, texts, and movements within the Ancient, Middle, and Renaissance periods	Ex.1 Understand the history of representative epics as oral or written compositions	6	2		8	
		Identify conventional literary genres, elements, and devices	Ex.2 Identify major characters and figures that appear in more than one text	6	2		8	
		Employ discipline specific vocabulary in order to recognize the relationship between form and content	Ex. 3 Apply genre characteristics to representative texts	4	4		8	1
		Relate literary or cultural concepts, principles, terms, strategies, and styles to a range of literature	Ex.4 Identify and connect literary or cultural concepts as they directly relate to representative texts	5	3		8	
	Read critically and analytically	Analyze, evaluate, interpret, synthesize representative texts from the Eastern and Western traditions and relate them to their literary and cultural contexts	Ex.5 Relate cultural qualities of a hero to a representative character	3	2	2	7	1
		Compare and contrast major literary figures, their situations, decisions	Ex.6 Compare the Eastern depiction of fate, virtue, and heroism to the Western depiction in representative texts	2	3	2	7	1
		Make connections among various periods, texts, authors, and characters	Ex.7 Differentiate between concepts, such as absolutism and relativism, using examples from representative texts	3	2	2	7	1
		Evaluate the ideas presented in a text, their implications, and their relationship to ideas beyond the text	Ex.8 Evaluate characters' decisions and actions in the context of their various cultures and worldviews	2	2	3	7	1
	Construct informed, organized, and coherent written responses to literary texts	Formulate a central interpretive idea about the texts; Develop ideas logically and coherently with adequate supporting textual examples; Present ideas clearly and concisely; Observe the standard conventions of formatting, citation, grammar, and punctuation	Written Composition (See Constructed Response Rubric)					

Course Effectiveness

"The following table shows the students mean scores for the first two semesters that the redesigned course was taught for all the points used to calculate the students' grades. Because the means are similar and the standard deviations are large, a statistical significance was not found for any pairs of semesters even though the drop, fail, and withdrawal rate decreased by 5 percent in the fall and 13 percent in the spring. One of the department's goals is to lower the DFW rates and raise the mean scores each year, which will make it likely that, in addition to the DFW percentage improvements, a significant statistical difference will be found in the mean and standard deviation, providing additional support for attributing student improvement to course redesign."[4]

	Semester	Section	N	Mean	Std. Deviation
Original	06 spring	.007	150	68.99	26.13
	06 fall	.002	144	69.18	25.48
	07 spring	.007	143	72.23	21.63
Redesign	07 fall	.002	153	69.34	26.73
	08 spring	.006	64	61.70	35.67
		.007	145	76.20	27.05

Student Reaction to the Redesigned Course

"The following table shows the results of a survey administered to students in Fall-07 N-Gen courses that asked the students the following question: *If you were to start this course over again, would you prefer a traditional face-to-face format (FTF), or would you prefer the N-Gen redesign format you are experiencing? Please tell why.*

The survey was administered during the last month of the semester. Student status as successful in the course (S = A,B,C) or unsuccessful (U = DFW) was entered by the instructor at the end of the course.

The following table shows the student preferences for course format plus the preferences by the successful and unsuccessful categories. The values in parentheses are percentages.

Student course format preferences with percentages of success

Semester	Course	Preferred N-gen	Preferred FTF	Total Number Success	Total Number Unsuccessful	Success preferred N-Gen	Success preferred FTF	Unsuccess preferred N-Gen	Unsuccess preferred FTF
Fall2007	ENG 2210	48(.70)	21(.30)	59(.86)	10(.14)	41(.69)	18(.31)	7(.70)	3(.30)
Spg2008 ENG	2210	66 (.69)	30 (.31)	89 (.93)	7 (.07)	60 (.67)	29 (.33)	6 (.86)	1 (.14)

The results show that a significantly higher percentage of students preferred an N-Gen course format versus a traditional FTF course format. Additionally, the data show that a significantly higher percentage of successful students preferred the N-Gen course format than unsuccessful students. A higher percentage of the unsuccessful students also preferred the N-Gen courses.

Student Comments

Student comments as to why they preferred an N-Gen format versus an FTF format were also collected and categorized by the primary reasons for the student's choice. Four "reason-categories" emerged for the N-Gen format and four for the FTF format. For the N-Gen course format, the reasons fell into the following categories: Pace (liked that they could control the rate at which they absorbed information); Flexibility (liked that they could do assignments whenever and wherever they wanted); Learning (found it easier to learn content when it is internet based); Practice (there were more opportunities to practice and learn).

For the FTF course format, the reasons fell into the following categories: Manage (students needed a structure so that they wouldn't procrastinate); Learning (found it easier to learn content when format is FTF); People (a preference for FTF interactions); Technical (student had difficulties with computers, network, and technology used).

The following table shows a typical comment for each of the reason categories for the format preference of N-Gen versus FTF. Also shown is the number of comments per category. There are 128 comments from students who prefer N-Gen format and 44 comments from students who prefer FTF format that clearly fit the categories in Table 2, for a total of 172 comments. The total number of comments collected is 182. Most of the non-included remaining 10 comments combined so much information that it wasn't possible to assign the comment to one specific category."[5]

Typical comments and counts for reasons for choosing N-Gen versus FTF

Format	Reason Category	Typical Comment
N-Gen	Pace (6)	I liked that I could do most of the work at my own pace when I had time to do it. If I wanted to go a little slower, I could.
	Flexibility (58)	This course allowed me to work out my hectic schedule. Being able to submit quizzes and stuff online made my life easier.
	Learning (58)	I like to learn from a bunch of different sources at once and this course really allowed me the chance to do that. You got stuff from online sources and you got some face to face interaction and I think I ended up learning more in this course than I would have otherwise.
	Practice (6)	I always liked the fact that you could go back and take the quizzes over and over again until you got them right. I really feel like that helped me a lot in the class.
FTF	Manage (10)	I prefer a traditional face-to-face lecture because I would often forget about online assignments and I think my grade suffered. I need more structure in my courses so, I need to come to campus more often!
	Learning (19)	I seem to absorb the information better in a traditional class format when I'm taking notes during a lecture. It just suits my learning style better.
	People (10)	I can't seem to learn without a teacher lecturing to me and me taking notes. Maybe it something about the interaction in the communication. I guess I just like being around people.
	Technical (5)	I don't trust submitting my quizzes online. The internet didn't seem to be reliable. Sometimes the website would be slow or wouldn't work at all. SO frustrating!

Unexpected Benefits

One of the unexpected benefits of engaging in course redesign was the opportunity to mentor masters and doctoral students as they began grading and teaching classes for the first time. The course materials and pedagogical approach provided a perfect context from which to introduce teaching fellows to teaching the literature of the period. The teaching fellows use the curriculum materials created during the redesign project and lead some of the small group sessions. The instructor models the pedagogical techniques used in the class and demonstrates best teaching practices. In some sense, the instructor is showing them how to use technology in meaningful ways, aligned with measurable outcomes, in the World Literature classroom. Previously, there was no method in the department available to provide this level of training to graduate students.

How can this course be modified or adopted by another instructor?

Other instructors have already adopted the assessment plan and the grading rubrics used in this course. The rubrics, in particular, are general enough that they can be used in any literature class and have also been adapted for other humanities courses, including the U.S. History survey courses.

C O N C L U S I O N

I received an email recently from a Faculty Professional Developmental List-Serve to which I belong about YouTube videos of students demonstrating methods they have used to cheat on exams. "Cheat and Never Get Caught" can be viewed at http://ie.youtube.com/watch?v=8KZwFLtMwsY&feature=related, and once you have opened this link, a dozen more similar videos will appear as linkable options on the right-hand side of the page.

"Cheat and Never Get Caught" is a fairly-high end production, well made and produced with a great degree of sophistication. I was enthralled watching it for several reasons:
- Clearly someone with a great deal of talent and technical skill produced this video.
- The content was well organized, witty, and got its message across in a persuasive manner.
- The producer (or someone close to him or her) had invented a highly ingenious means of cheating—and likely never getting caught.

In essence, the video producer had used the very high-level critical thinking skills in producing this video (and the method of cheating described) that we want our students to master.

Not all the videos I accessed were that thoughtfully produced nor were all the methods for cheating as ingenious, but all shared at least one common quality for me: they made me ask, "WHY?" Why were apparently bright, articulate students spending their time inventing ways to cheat? I came up with a list of possible reasons:

1) Schoolwork is so routine and mundane that these bright students need an inventive outlet.

2) The video producer could gain world-wide fame and the eternal gratitude of all students everywhere.

3) The current school structure rewards memorization and recall and these can be enhanced through particular methods of cheating.

4) Developing a "fool-proof" means of cheating mimics the scientific method— students hypothesize a method of cheating, construct it, test it, then refine it. They are using YouTube to share their findings with the larger community.

5) Students crave real learning! They are sending us a message!

The question we should be asking is not WHY are students cheating but *why are we creating learning experiences that are so superficial that cheating is even considered?* Our job as teachers is to construct real, meaningful learning experiences and then assess those experiences in ways that encourage mastery. Our students want to learn, but most have been conditioned to not expect real learning to take place within school walls. For them, real learning takes place elsewhere—like on YouTube.

We must change our expectations and create classrooms where real, deep, relevant learning is the norm. Expect more from your students—they will live up to your expectations. If you expect little from them, they will deliver little to you in return.

A recent article in *Liberal Education* encourages institutions to frame their approach to education using the "Student as Scholar" model. The authors—Hodge, Lepore, Pasquesi, Hirsh—argue that "developing the Student as Scholar Model requires a fundamental shift in how the whole undergraduate experience is structured and imagined," requiring "that a culture of inquiry-based learning be infused throughout the entire liberal arts curriculum, starting with the very first day of college and reinforced in every classroom and program." The authors believe that "a truly extraordinary student experience" is possible if institutions and their instructors will create learning paradigms, "establishing goals, assessing outcomes, and making learning an active process."[1]

This mandate is in line with a recent call from the Department of Education. A recent Commission appointed by Secretary Spellings spent more than a year looking at the state of higher education in the United States and determined that it has become

> . . . what, in the business world, would be called a mature enterprise: increasingly risk-averse, at times self-satisfied, and unduly expensive. It is an enterprise that has yet to address the fundamental issues of how academic programs and institutions must be transformed to serve the changing educational needs

of a knowledge economy. It has yet to successfully confront the impact of globalization, rapidly evolving technologies, an increasingly diverse and aging population, and an evolving marketplace characterized by new needs and new paradigms.[2]

The Commissioners argued that higher education risks obsolescence if it fails to notice that the world has changed. "Without serious self-examination and reform," they say, "institutions of higher education risk falling in to the same trap [disappearing]."[3]

The Commission has offered ambitious goals, reflecting their expectations from higher education:
- "We want a world-class higher-education system that creates new knowledge, contributes to economic prosperity and global competitiveness, and empowers citizens;
- We want a system that is accessible to all Americans, throughout their lives;
- We want postsecondary institutions to provide high-quality instruction while improving their efficiency in order to be more affordable to the students, taxpayers, and donors who sustain them;
- We want a higher-education system that gives Americans the workplace skills they need to adapt to a rapidly changing economy;
- We want postsecondary institutions to adapt to a world altered by technology, changing demographics and globalization, in which the higher-education landscape includes new providers and new paradigms, from for-profit universities to distance learning."[4]

The goals the Commission has set are lofty and will require a complete re-think of the educational system. That "re-think" may well begin within the walls of the classroom with instructors redesigning their courses for transformative learning.

I was hanging out in a common area of one of our campus buildings the other day and was casually dressed—blending in, I thought, more than usual. Two students were hunched over a table flipping through spiral notebooks, creating flashcards of terms. "I hate this class!" said the student in green. "My professor is *crazy*! There's no way I can remember all this stuff!"

"I know," responded the other, "but I don't think you have to. My professor highlighted all the things we have to remember on his PowerPoint notes. He said that if it wasn't highlighted, we didn't need it. It was—'for your information.'"

"What does that mean?"

"I don't know. I just know that means it won't be on the test."

"I'm failing. How are you doing?"

"I'm making a 69."

"Wow—you're doing great. Is your prof easy? I gotta figure out who to take 1060 from because I ain't taking it from this crazy lady."

"Yeah, he's easy."

I'll admit that I was shocked listening to them, but I'm not sure why. I *know* that most students pick faculty based on ease—wanting to do as little as possible for the maximum grade. All faculty know this—we spend a significant amount of our down-time together railing against just this attitude.

And we like to blame the students. "I wasn't like that," I argue. "I wanted to learn for the sake of learning!" Certainly I like to think of myself in that light and for the most part it's true, but if I'm honest with myself there were instructors that bored me near to death. I just wanted to get the required credit hour over with and move on with my life. Almost always, though, it wasn't the topic or discipline that was so unbearable but the way the material was approached.

These students were behaving in exactly the manner in which we have trained them. They are living up to the expectations we set for them. As John Tagg states in the Learning Paradigm College, "We need to make colleges and universities the kinds of places where undergraduate students learn the power of learning, and relearn the power of education. That means making them places where we, along with our students, unlearn the false lessons that the calcified and nonfunctional patterns of schooling have taught us, lessons that serve us all so poorly."[5]

Course redesign is one of the best places for an instructor to begin this process. Faculty can engage in a square-one rethink of how to best teach their discipline to their students. After working through this book, the instructor is prepared to transform his or her classroom, having aligned student learning outcomes, assessments, and teaching strategies, with an emphasis on active learning. The instructor is no longer thinking about teaching, but instead is focused on student learning. Teaching is not just the transmission of knowledge—it is the dissemination of passion and a way of viewing the world. It is a means of engaging others in our enthusiasms.

What if students everywhere truly engaged in learning? The artificial barriers built over decades would come tumbling down, replaced with an osmosis-like structure where the lines between academics, play, and business would disappear. Instructors have an opportunity to lead their institutions into the 21st century, demanding innovation and flexibility for their students. Course redesign offers the promise and possibility that we can collectively think about better ways to engage our students today and in the future.

E N D N O T E S

Introduction

[1] Learn more about the Croquet Alliance and Open Source Consortium at http://www.opencroquet.org/index.php/Main_Page.

[2] Landmark research in this area was conducted by Neil Howe and William Strauss. Neil Howe and William Strauss, *Millenials go to College: Strategies for a New Generation on Campus*, (Washington, D.C.: American Association of Collegiate Registrars & Life Course Associates, 2003).

[3] Mark Dembo, "Reaching Generation Y," *Public Relations Tactics* 7 (5): 20-25; W. R. Habley, "First-Year Students: The Year 2000" in *First Year Academic Advising: Patterns in the Present, Pathways to the Future* eds. M. L. and G. L. Kramer (South Carolina: University of South Carolina, National Resource Center for the Freshman Year Experience and Students in Transition, 1995): 3-25; J. L. Levere, "A Generation Shaped by Digital Media Presents Fresh Marketing Challenges, A Study Finds, *New York Times*, January 29, 1999; R Zemke, C. Raines, B. Filipczak, *Generations at Work: Managing the Clash of Veterans, Boomers, Xers, and Nexters in your Workplace.* (New York: Amacon, Ama Publications, 2000).

[4] Reynol Junco and Jeanna Mastrodicasa, *Connecting to the Net Generation: What Higher Education Professionals Need to Know about Today's Students* (Maryland: NASPA, March 29, 2007).

[5] Marc Prensky "Digital Natives, Digital Immigrants," from *On the Horizon* 9 (5) (MCB University Press, 2001), 1.

[6] Ibid, 2-4.

[7] Ibid, 3.

[8] Marshal McLuhan, "The Invisible Environment: The Future of an Erosion," *Perspecta* 11 (1967): 163-167.

[9] John Harris, "Brief History of American Academic Credit System: A Recipe for Incoherence in Student Learning," Report written for the Department of Education, Sanford University, September 2002.

[10] John Dewey, "My Pedagogic Creed' *The School Journal*, 14 (1897): 77-80.

[11] David Williamson Shaffer, *How Computer Games Help Children Learn* (New York: Palgrave MacMillan, 2006), ix.

[12] Ibid, 2 (quote); Thomas Friedman, *The World is Flat: A Brief History of the Twenty-First Century* (New York: Farrar, Straus, and Giroux, 2005).

[13] The Massachusetts Foundation for the Humanities, http://www.mfh.org/foundation/human.htm

[14] National Commission on Excellence in Education, "A Nation at Risk: The Imperative for Educational Reform," (1983), National Commission on Excellence in Education, http://www.ed.gov/pubs/NatAtRisk/index.html.

[15] Michael Wesch is an Assistant Professor of Cultural Anthropology at Kansas State University and has created a "World Simulation" for use in large lecture introductory Cultural Anthropology classes. The video can be found at: http://www.youtube.com/watch?v=dGCJ46vyR9o.

[16] Carl Wieman quoted in Justin Pope, "Colleges Cope With Bigger Classes," Washington *Post*, November 25, 2007.

[17] Kay M. McClenney, "Community Colleges Perched at the Millennium: Perspectives on Innovation, Transformation, and Tomorrow," *Leadership Abstracts*, 11 (August, 1998): 17.

Chapter One

[1] Lynne V. Cheney, "American Memory: A report on the Humanities in the Nation's Public School." National Endowment for the Humanities, Washington, DC, 1987.

[2] J. Carleton Bell and David F. McCollulm, "A Study of the Attainments of Pupils in United States History," *Journal of Educational Psychology* 8 (1917): 257-74; Diane Ravitch and Chester Finn, Jr., *What do our 17-Year-olds Know? A Report on the Frist National Assessment of History and Literature* (New York, 1987), *New York Times*, May 2, 1976; *New York Times Magazine*, May 3, 1942.

[3] John Tagg, *The Learning Paradigm College* (Massachusetts: Anker Publishing Company, 2003), xii

[4] John Bowden and Ference Marton, *The University of Learning* (London: Kogan Page, 1998), 13.

[5] Paul Ramsden, *Learning to Teach in Higher Education*, (New York: Routledge, 1992).

[6] U.S. Department of Education: A Report of the Commission Appointed by Secretary of Education Margaret Spellings, "A Test of Leadership: Charting the Future of U.S. Higher Education," September 2006, U.S. Department of Education, http://www.ed.gov/about/bdscomm/list/hiedfuture/reports/pre-pub-report.pdf.

[7] Frost quoted in Jay Parini, *The Art of Teaching* (NY: Oxford, 2005), 85.

[8] University of California, Berkeley, "Reinventing Large Enrollment Courses," U.C. Berkeley, http://education.berkeley.edu/accreditation/ee_essays_2.html

[9] Donald Wulff, Jody D. Nyquist, and Robert D. Abbott, "Students' Perceptions of Large Classes," in *Teaching Large Classes Well,* ed. Maryellen Weimer (San Francisco: Jossey-Bass, 1987), 17-30.

[10] Joe Cuseo, "The Empirical Case Against Large Class Size: Adverse Effects on the Teaching, Learning, and Retention of First-Year Students," Policy Center on the First Year of College, http://www.brevard.edu/fyc/listserv/remarks/cuseoclasssize.pdf. Acquired September 10, 2008.

[11] W. J. McKeachie, *Teaching Tips: Strategies, Research, and Theory for College and University Teachers* 10th ed. (Boston: Houston Mifflin, 1999); F. Costin, "Lecturing Versus Other Methods of Teaching: A Review of Research," *British Journal of Educational Technology,* 3 (1972): 4-30; J. B. Cuseo, *Cooperative Learning: A Pedagogy for Addressing Contemporary Challenges and Critical Issues in Higher Education* (Oklahoma: New Forums Press, 1996); Lion F. Gardiner, "Redesigning Higher Education: Producing Dramatic Gains in Student Learning," ASHE_ERIC higher Education Report No. 7, (Washington, DC: George Washington University, 1994).

[12] Hamilton Holt, " . . . Denies their Conferences Turn into Lectures," *The Daily Princetonian* (January 22, 1931); Holt quoted in William Honan, "Whither College Lectures?," *New York Times* (August 14, 2002).

[13] Lion F. Gardiner, "Redesigning Higher Education."

[14] David Johnson, Roger Johnson, and Karl Smith, *Active Learning: Cooperation in the College Classroom* 2nd ed. (Minnesota: Interaction Books, 1998).

[15] George Kuh, John H. Schuh, and Elizabeth Whitt, *Involving Colleges: Successful Approaches to Fostering Student Learning and Development Outside the Classroom* (California: Jossey-Bass, 1991), 362.

Chapter Two

[1] Learn more about the Shakespeare authorship debate at Absolute Shakespeare, http://absoluteshakespeare.com/trivia/authorship/authorship.htm.

[2] D. A. McDonnell, D. N. Steer, and K. D. Owens, "Assessment and Active Learning Strategies for Introductory Geology Courses," *Journal of Geoscience Education* 51 (1996): 205-216.

[3] M.D. Sundberg, M. L. Dini, and E. Li, "Decreasing Course Content Improves Students' Comprehension of Science and Attitudes Toward Science in Freshman Biology," *Journal of Research in Science Teaching* 31 (1994): 679-639.

[4] Jay McTighe and Grant Wiggins, *Understanding by Design* (New Jersey: Merrill Prentice Hall, 1998), 5.

[5] Ibid, 76.

[6] L. Dee Fink, "A Self-Directed Guide to Designing Courses for Significant Learning," University of Virginia, Teaching Resource Center, http://trc.virginia.edu/Workshops/2004/Fink_Designing_Courses_2004.pdf.

Chapter Three

[1] See for example, Joseph D. Novak and D. B. Gowin, *Learning how to Learn* (Cambridge University Press, 1984).

[2] Benjamin Bloom, *Taxonomy of Educational Objectives* (New York: Longmans, 1954).

[3] Lorin Anderson, et. al., *A Taxonomy for Learning, Teaching, and Assessing: A Revision of Bloom's Taxonomy of Educational Objectives* (New York: Longman, 2001).

[4] Robert M. Gagne, *The Conditions of Learning*, 4th ed. (New York: Holt, Rinehart, and Winston, 1985).

[5] Ibid, 44. McTighe and Wiggins developed the six facets of understanding to align with Costa and Liebmann's Intellectual Engagement Factors. Costa and Liebmann (1997)

[6] Elliot Eisner, *The Art of Educational Evaluation: A Personal View* (London: Falmer Press, 1985).

Chapter Four

[1] See the 2003 National Assessment of Adult Literacy, Institute of Education Sciences, http://nces.ed.gov/naal/.

[2] U.S. Department of Education, "A Report of the Commission Appointed by Secretary of Education Margaret Spellings: A Test of Leadership: Charting the Future of U.S. Higher Education," U.S. Department of Education, http://www.ed.gov/about/bdscomm/list/hiedfuture/reports/pre-pub-report.pdf.

[3] Sally Brown and Peter Knight, *Assessing Learners in Higher Education* (London: Kogan Page, 1994).

[4] Diana Oblinger, "Making the Grade: The Role of Assessment in Authentic Learning," ELI Paper 1. (Educause, 2008) 1-16, Educause Connect, http://connect.educause.edu/Library/ELI/MakingtheGradeTheRoleofAs/45771?time=1221847503.

[5] L. Dee Fink, "A Self-Directed Guide to Designing Courses for Significant Learning," University of Virginia, Teaching Resource Center, http://trc.virginia.edu/Workshops/2004/Fink_Designing_Courses_2004.pdf., 13.

[6] Ibid.

[7] P. Nightingale, I. T.Wiata, S. Toohey, G. Ryan, C. Hughes, D. Magin, "Assessing Learning in Universities Professional Development Centre" (New South Wales: University of New South Wales, Australia: 1996). See also, S. Brown, C. Rust, G. Gibbs, "Strategies for Diversifying Assessment Oxford Centre for Staff Development," (UK: Oxford Brooks University, 1994).

[8] For more detailed information on writing rubrics and outcome-based assessments in general, see Ronald S. Carriveau, "Writing Outcome-Based Assessments Handbook," (Denton, TX: Center for Learning Enhancement, Assessment, and Redesign, University of North Texas), 2007.

[9] Peter Airasian, *Classroom Assessment* (NY: McGraw-Hill, 1991); Robert L. Linn and N. E. Gronlund, *Measurement and Assessment in Teaching* 7th ed. (NJ: Prentice Hall, 1995).

Chapter Five

[1] John D. Bransford, Ann L. Brown, and Rodney R. Cocking, eds. *How People Learn* (Washington, D.C.: The National Academies Press, 1999), 6; John Tagg, *The Learning Paradigm College* (MA: Anker Publishing Company, Inc., 2003), 62.

[2] Paul Ramsden, *Learning to Teach in Higher Education* (New York: Routledge, 1992), 53.

[3] Ibid, 45.

[4] Ibid, 60.

[5] Arthur Chickering and Zelda Gamson, *Applying the Seven Principles for Good Practice in Undergraduate Education* (NJ: Jossey-Bass, 1991); Christopher J. Lucas and John W. Murray, *New Faculty: A Practical Guide for Academic Beginners* (NY: Palgrave Macmillan, 2002),73.

[6] Wingfield, Sue Stewart and Gregory S. Black, "Active Versus Passive Course Designs: The Impact on Student Outcomes." *Journal of Education for Business* 61 (Nov.-Dec. 2005): 119-25; Scott D. Wurdinger, *Using Experiential Learning in the Classroom: Practical Ideas for All Educators* (Lanham, MD: Scarecrow Education, 2005).

[7] This chapter has been prepared with the assistance of Cynthia Beard. Beard is a Research Associate at the Center for Learning Enhancement, Assessment, and Redesign at the University of North Texas. The information related to specific kinds of active learning has been modified from original content created by Beard and is used here with her permission.

[8] Clyde Freeman Herreid, "What Makes a Good Case? Some Basic Rules of Good Storytelling Help Teachers Generate Student Excitement in the Classroom," National Center for Case Study Teaching in Science, http://ublib.buffalo.edu/libraries/projects/cases/teaching/good-case.html. See also Suzanne E. Wade, ed. *Inclusive Education: A Casebook and Readings for Prospective and Practicing Teachers* (Mahwah, NJ: Lawrence Erlbaum Associates, 2000); Howard Barrows, "Strategies for Using Case Studies in Teaching and Learning." *SEATEC Case Study Forum* Short Paper (25 February 1999), South East Advanced Technological Education Consortium, http://www.nscc.edu/seatec/pages_resources/forum_papers_pdf/Barrows2.pdf; and Daniel Fasko Jr., "Case Studies and Methods in Teaching and Learning," Paper presented at the Annual Meeting of the Society of Educators and Scholars, Louisville, Kentucky, April 2003.

[9] Herreid, "What Makes a Good Case?

[10] Stephen D. Brookfield and Stephen Preskill, *Discussion as a Way of Teaching: Tools and Techniques for Democratic Classrooms* (CA: Jossey-Bass Publishers, 1999), 114-15.

[11] Morry Van Ments, *The Effective Use of Role-play: Practical Techniques for Improving Learning*, 2nd ed. (London: Kogan Page, 1983), 30.

[12] For more information see Ray A. Burnstein and Leon M. Lederman, "Using Wireless Keypads in Lecture Classes," *The Physics Teacher* 39 (January 2001): 8-11l;

Chrysanthe Demetry, "Use of Educational Technology to Transform the 50-Minute Lecture: Is Student Response Dependent on Learning Style?" *Proceedings of the 2005 American Society for Engineering Education Annual Conference and Exposition*, Worcester Polytechnic Institute, http://www.wpi.edu/Academics/ATC/Collaboratory/Stories/ASEE05demetry.pdf; and Eugene Judson and Daiyo Sawada, "Learning from Past and Present: Electronic Response Systems in College Lecture Halls," *Journal of Computers in Mathematics and Science Teaching* 21 (2002): 167-81.

[13] Jeremy Roschelle, William R. Penuel, Louise Yarnall, Nicole Shechtman, and Deborah Tatar, "Handheld Tools that 'Informate' Assessment of Student Learning in Science: A Requirements Analysis," *Journal of Computer Assisted Learning* 21 (2005): 190-203.

[14] M. Beckman, "Collaborative Learning: Preparation for the Workplace and Democracy" *College Teaching* 38 (1990): 128-133.; A. W. Chickering and Z. F. Gamson, eds., *"Applying the Seven Principles for Good Practice in Undergraduate Education." New Directions for Teaching and Learning*, (CA: Jossey Bass, 1991), 63-69; K. G. Collier, "Peer-Group Learning in Higher Education: The Development of Higher-order Skills." *Studies in Higher Education* 5(1), (1980): 55-62; J. Cooper and Associates, *Cooperative Learning and College Instruction.* (CA: Institute for Teaching and Learning, California State University, 1990); D. W. Johnson, R. T. Johnson, and K. A. Smith, *Cooperative Learning: Increasing College Faculty Instructional Productivity*, ASHE-FRIC Higher Education Report No.4.(Washington, D.C.: School of Education and Human Development, George Washington University, 1991); W. J. McKeachie, P. R. Pintrich, Y. Lin, and D. A. F. Smith, *Teaching and Learning in the College Classroom: A Review of the Research Literature* (Ann Arbor: National Center for Research to Improve Postsecondary Teaching and Learning, University of Michigan, 1986).

[15] L. K. Michaelson and R. H. Black, "Building Learning Teams: The Key to Harnessing the Power of Small Groups in Higher Education," in *Collaborative Learning: A Sourcebook for Higher Education* vol. 2 (PA: National Center on Postsecondary Teaching, Learning, and Assessment, 1994): 65-81.

[16] Frank Lyman, "Think-Pair-Share: An Expanding Teaching Technique," MAA-CIE Cooperative News 1 (1981): 1-2.

[17] Michaelson and Black, "Building Learning Teams."

[18] L. Dee Fink, "Beyond Small Groups: Harnessing the Extraordinary Power of Learning Teams," in *Team-Based Learning: A Transformative Use of Small Groups*, ed. Larry K. Michaelsen, Arletta Bauman Knight, and L. Dee Fink (Connecticut and London: Praeger, 2002), 3-25.

[19] Ibid.; Larry K. Michaelson, "Getting Started with Team-Based Learning," in *Team-Based Learning*, 27-51; Larry K. Michaelson, "Creating Effective Assignments: A Key Component of Team-Based Learning," in *Team-Based Learning*, 53-75.

[21] Michaelson, "Getting Started with Team-Based Learning."

[22] Ibid.

[23] A. F. Grasha, *Teaching with Style* (PA: Alliance, 1996), 41.

[24] R. M. Felder and R. Brent, "Understanding Student Differences," *Journal of Engineering Education* 94 (2005): 57-72; Felder and E. R. Henriques, "Learning and Teaching Styles in Foreign and Second Language Education," *Foreign Language Annals* 28 (1995): 21-31.

[25] B. K. Beyer, "Critical Thinking: What is it?," *Social Education* 49 (1985): 270-276; A. L. Costa, ed., *Developing Minds: A Resource book for Teaching Thinking* (VA: Association for Supervision and Curriculum Development, 1985).

Chapter Six

—no notes

Chapter Seven

[1] This case study was prepared by holding an interview with Beard in October 2008 and through materials available on her N-Gen website at http://qep.unt.edu. Any omissions or misrepresentations of the course are my own.

Chapter Eight

[1] This case study was written in conjunction with and from materials provided by Dr. Denise Baxter. Please see her portion of the N-Gen Course Redesign™ website for materials cited here, plus additional resources related to this course. http://qep.unt.edu. Any misrepresentations of the course are my own.

[2] Kelly Donahue-Wallace and Denise Baxter, "Defining the "Other" in a DFW Museum Case Study©." Case Study created 2007 and owned by Donahue-Wallace and Baxter.

Chapter Nine

[1] This case study was prepared by holding an interview with Dr. Tracey Gau in July 2008 and with materials available on her N-Gen website at http://qep.unt.edu. Any omissions or misrepresentations of the course are my own.

[2] Tracey Gau, World Literature I, Center for Learning Enhancement, Assessment, and Redesign, UNT, http://qep.unt.edu.

[3] Ibid.

[4] Tracey Gau, "Student Assessment and Evaluation for N-Gen World Literature I," Center for Learning Enhancement, Assessment, and Redesign, UNT, http://qep.unt.edu, 7.

[5] Ibid, 13-14.

Conclusion

[1] David Hodge, Paul Lepore, Kira Pasquesi, and Marissa Hirsch, "It Takes a Curriculum: Preparing Students for Research & Creative Work," *Liberal Education* (Summer 2008): 8-9.

[2] U.S. Department of Education: A Report of the Commission Appointed by Secretary of Education Margaret Spellings, "A Test of Leadership: Charting the Future of U.S. Higher Education," September 2006, U.S. Department of Education, http://www.ed.gov/about/bdscomm/list/hiedfuture/reports/pre-pub-report.pdf, ix.

[3] Ibid.

[4] Ibid, viii.

[5] John Tagg, *The Learning Paradigm College* (MA: Anker Publishing Company, Inc., 2003), 342-343.